CRITICAL PERSPECTIVES ON
GERRYMANDERING

ANALYZING THE ISSUES

CRITICAL PERSPECTIVES ON
GERRYMANDERING

Edited by Jennifer Peters

Enslow Publishing

101 W. 23rd Street
Suite 240
New York, NY 10011
USA

enslow.com

Published in 2020 by Enslow Publishing, LLC
101 W. 23rd Street, Suite 240, New York, NY 10011

Library of Congress Cataloging-in-Publication Data

Names: Peters, Jennifer, editor.
Title: Critical perspectives on gerrymandering / edited by Jennifer Peters.
Description: New York : Enslow Publishing, 2020. | Series: Analyzing the
issues | Audience: 7-12. | Includes bibliographical references and index.
Identifiers: LCCN 2018022674| ISBN 9781978503281 (library bound) | ISBN
9781978504981 (paperback)
Subjects: LCSH: Gerrymandering—United States—Juvenile literature.
Classification: LCC JK1341 .C876 2019 | DDC 328.73/073455—dc23
LC record available at https://lccn.loc.gov/2018022674

Printed in the United States of America

To Our Readers: We have done our best to make sure all website addresses
in this book were active and appropriate when we went to press. However,
the author and the publisher have no control over and assume no
liability for the material available on those websites or on any websites
they may link to. Any comments or suggestions can be sent by email to
customerservice@enslow.com.

Excerpts and articles have been reproduced with the permission of the
copyright holders.

Photo Credits: Cover AFP/Getty Images; cover and interior pages graphics
Thaiview/Shutterstock.com (cover top, pp. 3, 6–7), gbreezy/Shutterstock.
com (magnifying glass), Ghornstern/Shutterstock.com (chapter openers).

CONTENTS

INTRODUCTION

Gerrymandering is a hot topic in the United States, and it's an important issue each year as we near election season. Gerrymandering is the practice of drawing district voting boundaries in a way that influences who can win an election. Sometimes people draw boundaries to keep a particular race of people from having voting power, and other times they do it to keep a particular political party from winning. Other times, legislators use prisons to increase populations in a district and allow them to redraw the district boundaries to help them keep a seat even though the real voting population wouldn't support such boundary lines.

But is gerrymandering a problem? That's the question you'll try to answer as you read the articles in this book. Gerrymandering doesn't just target one group of people. Sometimes Republicans use redistricting maps to block voters of color who might not agree with their agenda from having the same voting power as others in the area. Other times, Democrats redraw the districts to keep conservative voters from voting them out of office. Gerrymandering can be used to block voters of different parties or races, and each is problematic for its own set of reasons and depending on whom you ask.

Gerrymandering is also often hard to prove, according to experts. It's not a simple problem, and it's equally complicated to solve. Everyone from local representatives to the justices of the United States Supreme Court has had a difficult time determining how much of a problem gerrymandering is and figuring out what can be done to stop it.

This problem has been a part of American politics for decades, but new theories and new evidence are coming along every day. From experts and academics to journalists and ordinary citizens, as well as court cases and government officials, you'll read a number of different takes on gerrymandering and what it means for democracy. As you read, consider each opinion and what it means for how democracy in America works. Then see if your opinions match up with the more recent Supreme Court rulings.

CHAPTER 1

WHAT ACADEMICS, EXPERTS, AND RESEARCHERS SAY

People have been studying and discussing gerrymandering for almost as long as Americans have been voting. The following articles will discuss not only whether gerrymandering is a problem, but how to fix it and what can be done to make redistricting more fair. You'll read about the mathematics behind redistricting, how districts are shaped, and what it means if nothing changes at all. As you read, you'll be asked to consider each method of redistricting and if or how each can improve upon the existing systems, and whether these new ways of thinking about voting can help make America's one person, one vote system more fair.

"REBOOTING THE MATHEMATICS BEHIND GERRYMANDERING," BY MOON DUCHIN AND PETER LEVINE, FROM *THE CONVERSATION*, OCTOBER 23, 2017

On Oct. 3, the Supreme Court heard oral arguments in a major case about the Wisconsin State Assembly districts.

In the U.S., we elect members to the House of Representatives and to state legislatures in a way that depends heavily on how states are divided into geographical districts. To win, you must simply get more votes than anyone else within your district's borders. Whoever draws those borders can have a profound effect on the outcome of an election.

In the Wisconsin case, the court is being asked to find – for the first time – a legal framework to control partisan gerrymandering. Their decision could limit the ability of a political party to draw maps to their own advantage.

However, partisan gerrymandering is just one way to rig election maps. With districting cases in contention around the country, citizens and experts alike need to better understand the math of redistricting and the choices involved in drawing electoral maps.

Our group of mathematicians is hosting free public workshops around the country. By improving understanding of the mathematics of redistricting, we hope to empower the public to engage in informed debates about district boundaries and composition.

AN OLD PROBLEM

The word "gerrymandering" derives from an 1812 political cartoon ridiculing a map drawn under Massachusetts Governor Elbridge Gerry. The cartoon suggested that one district in Boston's North Shore was shaped like a menacing reptile. (Gerry + Salamander = Gerrymander.)

That district actually isn't too bad by modern standards, either in terms of shape or demographic sophistication. Early 19th-century politicians lacked the tools of modern gerrymanderers.

Compare that with the current Seventh Congressional District in Pennsylvania, drawn by partisan actors armed with data on every registered voter. The district looks like fractal tumors oozing out from the suburbs of Philadelphia. Its only geometrically tame feature, a circular arc, comes from the Pennsylvania-Delaware state boundary!

But even more troubling than maps like these are those that push an agenda without such flagrant irregularities by, for instance, slicing a city into several pieces in order to dilute the votes of urban dwellers.

Each voter has numerous attributes, such as race, age, wealth and partisan preference. By clumping certain groups of voters together, line-drawers can give one particular group a substantial advantage over its competitors. This way, they might strengthen or weaken the representation of minority groups; protect incumbents or aid challengers; and make primary campaigns more or less likely.

The authorities who control the lines – usually state legislatures, but sometimes nonpartisan commissions or judges – are practicing political geometry, whether they think of it that way or not. They're carving up the population into pieces, and the shapes of those pieces matter.

FAIR MAPS ARE COMPLICATED

What makes a map fair? Since competing values are at stake, there's no purely mathematical solution.

The Constitution and subsequent court decisions suggest that each district should have very nearly equal populations. Other legally recognized principles tell us that districts should be connected; should try, when possible, to keep political subdivisions (like counties and cities) together; should respect natural geography; and should be "compact," or not too eccentrically shaped.

Many reasonable people believe that districts should be competitive and follow some guidelines of rough proportionality. In other words, the electoral representation shouldn't be too out of whack with the state's partisan breakdown, racial demographics and so on.

These values often conflict, and no technical analysis could decide which should matter more.

For the first time, technology is catching up to the redistricting problem. Teams of mathematicians, political scientists and computing experts at Duke and University of Illinois at Urbana-Champaign are building algorithms that can explore the enormous universe of possible districting maps.

These computer samplers generate thousands or millions of alternative maps in a given state. The maps can be used to assess whether a legislature's proposed plan is an outlier.

If a programmer is given specific rules for fair districting, they can then compare a given plan to a pool of valid alternative plans to figure out if its properties are too extreme.

COMPACTNESS

Let's look at just one possible constraint on plans: compactness.

Compactness is a legally recognized districting principle with a clear geometric flavor. It's intuitive that districts shouldn't have shapes that look manipulated or eccentric.

The more degrees of freedom the map-drawer has, the more control he or she exerts over the outcome. The ability to draw wild and wiggly shapes simply gives too much power to the person who wields the pen. Compactness is meant to constrain that.

But what does "compact" mean? At least 30 definitions can be found in the technical literature. Some invoke "isoperimetry," the idea that a district shouldn't have a very long boundary relative to its area. Some are based on "convexity," which means a straight line between two points in the district should stay in the district. Others are based on "dispersion," or the idea that districts shouldn't sprawl.

Looking back at Pennsylvania's Seventh District, you can see that it would fail all of these kinds of tests.

However, most existing definitions look at only the outline of the district on a map. They don't take into account the "guts" of the district, or how population clusters are lumped together by the line-drawers.

A square district that completely encompasses a city is very different from one that splits it right down the middle.

One simple idea is to represent districts as networks, where the nodes are population units like census blocks and the edges represent proximity or similarity. Ideas from discrete geometry may help us reinterpret compactness in a way that is much more relevant to the political realities.

But even with this new framing, compactness will still be in tension with other values. Citizens must consider the trade-offs between all the political ideals in play. Mathematical analysis can help clarify the choices.

EMPOWERING DEBATE

Shortly after the Supreme Court heard arguments on partisan gerrymandering, our group convened a conference in Madison, Wisconsin to discuss that case and the national scope of the gerrymandering challenge.

In a few weeks we are headed to Durham, North Carolina for public workshops that will center on the complex ongoing litigation there.

We hope to keep seeing a broad spectrum of people – mathematicians, political scientists, demographers, legal experts, coders, election officials, citizen advocates and more – coming together to figure out what is fair and how to measure it.

If you're interested, you can see public talks from our first workshop in August or join us at upcoming workshops around the country.

1. The authors discuss what districts should look like, both in the people who make them up as well as how they are drawn on a map. Of all of the things that should be taken into consideration when redistricting, what do you think are the three most important factors?

2. Take a look at your area's districting map and the data about the districts. If you were going to redraw your local district lines today, what would you do differently? What would you keep the same?

"REDISTRICTING SHOULD RESTORE REPRESENTATIVE DEMOCRACY," BY TODD EBERLY, FROM MARYLANDREPORTER.COM, SEPTEMBER 29, 2015

Professor Toddy Eberly of St. Mary's College of Maryland was scheduled to deliver this testimony to the Governor's Redistricting Reform Commission Tuesday night. The commission invited the political science professor and commentator to make a presentation.

First, let me thank the members of the Commission for welcoming me here today. The work that you are doing is critically important and the decisions that you make will affect the quality of governance in the state of Maryland

and perhaps inspire other states to take action that could ultimately improve the cause of fair and appropriate representation in every state.

I would like to thank Governor Hogan for fulfilling his promise to pursue reforms. And I would like to thank the Republican and the Democratic leadership in the General Assembly for agreeing to participate in this process by naming members to this commission.

IMPATIENT WITH PARTISANS

Let me start by admitting that I do not have much patience for dyed-in-the-wool partisans—Democrat or Republican. Folks who think that their party is dedicated to goodness and light and that the opposition party is evil incarnate really need to realize that there is nothing inherently good or evil about the Democratic or Republican Party. Yet die hard Democrats are convinced that Republicans are out to control the country through any and all means and die-hard Republicans are equally distrustful of Democrats.

In the end—the Democratic and Republican parties share the same goal—the acquisition of power and influence within government. And both parties will use whatever legal means are available to them to acquire that power.

In states dominated by Democrats, like Maryland and Illinois, Democrats use the redistricting process to game the system and boost party interests. Likewise, in states like Texas and North Carolina, Republicans do the same.

So a critique of Maryland's gerrymandered districts should not be viewed as an attack on the Democratic

Party. It's not. It is an attack on a process that encourages both parties to substitute their needs and their agenda for those of the people and the voters.

It's an attack on a process that subverts the very nature of representative government by allowing those in office to choose their voters instead of allowing voters to choose those who will serve in office.

THE ROLE OF REPRESENTATION AND THE HOUSE OF REPRESENTATIVES

I ask everyone to consider for a moment the issue of representation in America and the special role of the House of Representatives in our system of government.

Representation, or rather its lack, was a central cause of the Revolutionary War. As such, adequate and appropriate representation of the people was a central concern of the framers of our constitution.

At the time of our nation's founding, there were two dominant theories regarding Democracy and Representation. One, was the idea that only direct democracy could work. People could not expect others to represent them and represent them well. Two, was the idea that only good and virtuous men could serve as representatives. Given the impossibility posed by those two beliefs, representative government was dismissed as folly.

Men like James Madison and Alexander Hamilton disagreed. They believed that we could elect representatives. They even believed that personal virtue was not a necessary requirement for representation.

All that was needed was a mix of competing branches and accountability—accountability through elections. Nowhere would this be more true than in the House of Representatives.

No branch of the federal government was more important than the House for it alone was tasked with representing the people—not the states as in the Senate and not the nation as with the President—but the people.

Many early critics believed that Congress would simply become an institution that boosted the powerful few to a position of authority over weaker masses.

But Madison demanded, "who are to be the electors of these men and women?" It won't be the few or the powerful. It will be the masses. They will represent us, because they were elected by us.

And they will continue to be loyal to us and to represent us because we can fire them through elections.

Members of the House serve short terms in order to maximize the impact of accountability through elections. Of all the institutions of our national government, the House of Representatives was the one body most intended to embody democratic representation.

Well, that was 200 years ago.

PROTECTING INCUMBENTS AND PARTIES

No reasonable person could look at the Congressional District maps in Texas, North Carolina, Illinois, Pennsylvania, or Maryland—especially the 2nd, 3rd, or 4th districts in Maryland—and conclude that they were drawn to best represent the interests of the people or to boost accountability through elections

They were drawn to boost the protection of incumbents and to boost the prospects of the majority party in each state. It's that simple.

As Americans we should be outraged that both parties manipulate something as sacred as representation in the manner that they do—not only in the House of Representatives, but in state legislatures as well.

Gerrymandering ultimately subverts accountability through elections. And without accountability, we have no reason to expect representation.

Today, there are approximately 370-380 safe seats in the House of Representatives. Out of 435 seats, competition exists in about 60. In the rest, the incumbent is safe and protected—and largely unaccountable to anyone other than the small number of partisans who vote in primaries.

In safe seats the majority party is so protected there is no reason to listen to the demands or wishes of minority party voters in the district.

This, coupled with closed primaries, results in far more ideological candidates and representatives. These incumbents are so safe in the general election that their only real fear is a challenge from within their own party in a primary election. And since most states, including Maryland, hold closed primaries these "safe" incumbents are more concerned about pleasing the most partisan and ideological members of their party base—because those are the folks who cut checks and the folks who vote in primaries.

GOP DRIFTING RIGHT, DEMS DRIFTING LEFT

As a result, we have seen the Republican party drift ever rightward and the Democrats ever leftward. A once crucial and vibrant political center is now gone from Congress. As ever more Americans reject the party label our politics are driven ever more by two disparate and intransigent parties. As explored in both of the books I've written on American politics, partisan gerrymandering and incumbent protection contribute to this.

A member of Maryland's most recent redistricting commission defended the fact that so many of the state's districts contain parts of the Baltimore area by explaining that it's simply because so many of our incumbents live there. It's not about representation. It's about incumbent protection.

THE PROCESS IN THE STATES

In 36 states, the state legislatures are ultimately responsible for the redistricting plan, subject to approval by the state governor—totaling about 340 seats.

Seven states have one representative: Alaska, Delaware, Montana, North Dakota, South Dakota, Vermont and Wyoming—totaling 7 seats.

A hand full of states, with 88 seats—Arizona, California, Hawaii, Idaho, Minnesota, New Jersey and Washington—have rejected partisan gerrymandering in favor of a non-partisan process. This is what I would I like to see in Maryland. I want to see more states follow the lead of Iowa and California and make this a nonpartisan issue.

If Maryland were to add its 8 seats to the 88 now decided in a nonpartisan manner it would not be sufficient to make the difference between a Democratic or a Republican majority in the U.S. House. But it may inspire other states to act. There is much to be said for leading by example.

THE CALIFORNIA SYSTEM

In California, the district maps are drawn by a citizen's commission that convenes public hearings across the state. The commission consists of 5 Democrats, 5 Republicans and 4 Independent or Third Party members. For a map to be approved it must receive the support of 3 Democrats, 3 Republicans, and 3 of the Independent members. The Citizens' Commission must abide by these standards:

Population Equality: Districts must comply with the U.S. Constitution's requirement of "one person, one vote"

Federal Voting Rights Act: Districts must ensure an equal opportunity for minorities to elect a candidate of their choice

Geographic Contiguity: All areas within a district must be connected to each other, except for the special case of islands

Geographic Integrity: Districts shall minimize the division of cities, counties, local neighborhoods and communities of interests to the extent possible, without violating previous criteria. A community of interest is a contiguous population which shares common social and economic interests that should be included within a single district for purposes of its effective and fair representation.

Geographic Compactness: To the extent practicable, and where this does not conflict with previous criteria, districts must not bypass nearby communities for more distant communities.

In addition, incumbents, political candidates or political parties cannot be considered when drawing districts.

The results of this reform in California were nothing less than amazing. California's congressional districts were transformed from among the least competitive districts in the country to among the most competitive.

THE RESULTS IN CALIFORNIA

Consider—from 2002 to 2010, there were 265 House elections in California (53 seats x 5 elections)

In that time only one seat changed party hands (0.38%)

After California's redistricting plan and new map went into effect

14 of the 53 seats, 25%, are now competitive races

Of the 55 competitive seats nationally, California is home to 14…20 come from other states with non-partisan approaches; 14 result from partisan gerrymandering that has made the incumbent party vulnerable.

And for all of the controversy and all of the pushback by California's Democratic leaders, who feared that a fair process would simply mean the election of more Republicans, the process did nothing to boost the number of Republican held seats.

Democrats actually ended up with more seats AFTER the redistricting process.

BETTER REPRESENTATION

But the seats do a better job of representing the people and communities and the seats are far more competitive—meaning that representatives must worry about all of the voters in their district no just about partisan voters in a primary.

I have included the before and after maps from California and what you see under the new approach is a clear effort to respect existing community boundaries. [*Editor's note: Maps can be found with the original article online.*]

- Counties are not divided among multiple districts.
- Narrow, sprawling districts are pretty much gone
- Bizarre and oddly shaped districts in Los Angeles that cut across communities are now gone

California did the right thing. And the people of the state are better off and better represented.

THE RIGHT THING TO DO

Now, some folks have told me that so long as redistricting remains a partisan process and the GOP controls the process in states like Texas or North Carolina then it should be

OK for Democrats to manipulate the process in states where they dominate.

As a father, I've heard this argument many times. Except it usually goes like this "yea, but she started it," "did not," "did too." And it usually involves my 4- and 7-year-old daughters. It doesn't work for them and it doesn't work when it comes to restoring faith in politics.

I have little patience for folks who prefer excuses instead of reform, especially reform affecting something as important as representation in Congress. Redistricting reform is simply the right thing to do. And folks elected to represent the people of Maryland should not use the people of Texas, Pennsylvania or any other state as an excuse not to act.

1. One of the author's arguments is that redistricting in California, which was viewed as gerrymandering, actually created more competitive congressional races and resulted in the citizens of California being more accurately represented. Do you think what happened in California could be considered gerrymandering? Explain your response.

2. The author notes that redistricting should not consider politics or political party. What are things that you think also need to be ignored when redistricting? What are some things that should be considered?

CHAPTER 2

WHAT THE GOVERNMENT AND POLITICIANS SAY

Politicians are torn on the topic of gerrymandering. While many of them claim to find the practice unfair and un-American, just as many like it—at least when it helps them or their political party. Some people in the government believe that because gerrymandering is technically legal, it's acceptable for them to redraw district lines to serve themselves. Others believe that it should be up to the voters whether they're put into potentially gerrymandered districts. Sometimes the government makes laws to prevent gerrymandering, and in other places, it fights to allow it. You'll read about all the possible scenarios in the following articles.

"ARIZONA VOTERS CAN OVERRULE LEGISLATURE ON REDISTRICTING, HIGH COURT SAYS," BY SOYENIXE LOPEZ, FROM *CRONKITE NEWS*, JUNE 30, 2015

WASHINGTON – When voters approved the Arizona Independent Redistricting Commission they were reaffirming a "core principle" of government, the Supreme Court said Monday, "that voters should choose their representatives, not the other way around."

The court ruled 5-4 to uphold the commission that was approved by Arizona voters in 2000 as Proposition 106, in an attempt to curb gerrymandering of legislative and congressional districts.

The Arizona Legislature challenged the commission in 2012, after the most recent congressional district boundaries were drawn, claiming that the Constitution's elections clause put the power to draw congressional districts in the hands of the legislature.

Big month at the high court for Arizona
The Supreme Court took action an a slew of Arizona issues in June:

- Supreme Court lets stand ruling rejecting Arizona's immigrant bail ban
- Supreme Court sides with Gilbert pastor, strikes down town's sign law

- Even superheroes have limits: Court turns down Spider-Man toy inventor
- Obamacare ruling spares 127,000 in state with health care subsidies
- Arizona advocates vow to fight on as Supreme Court OKs same-sex marriage
- Court OKs use of lethal-injection drug used in botched Arizona execution
- Convicted former congressman Renzi's last-ditch appeal turned down
- States' bid to require citizenship proof for federal voters falls short
- Supreme Court agrees to hear new challenge to redistricting commission

But Justice Ruth Bader Ginsburg disagreed, writing for the majority that the elections clause cannot be invoked "to disempower the state's voters from serving as the legislative power for redistricting purposes."

"The people of Arizona turned to the initiative to curb the gerrymandering and, thereby, to ensure that members of Congress would have 'an habitual recollection of their dependence on the people,'" Ginsburg wrote, citing the Federalist Papers.

In the main dissent, Chief Justice John Roberts accused the majority of "deliberate constitutional evasion" by "revising 'the Legislature' to mean 'the people.'"

"The court's position has no basis in the text, structure or history of the Constitution, and it contradicts precedents from both Congress and the court," he wrote in a dissent joined by Justices Samuel Alito, Clarence Thomas and Antonin Scalia.

That sentiment was echoed Monday in a joint statement from Arizona House Speaker David Gowan and Senate President Andy Biggs, who said "clear constitutional design had been demolished in Arizona by five lawyers at the high court."

"We are disappointed that the Supreme Court has decided to depart from the clear language of the Constitution. The Framers selected the elected representatives of the people to conduct congressional redistricting," the statement said.

But voting-rights groups hailed the decision, which they said would be felt in any state where voters can petition issues to the ballot.

"Not only is it a victory for retaining this nonpartisan independent redistricting body, but it also strategically is an important victory for legislating through the ballot box," said Sam Wercinski, executive director for the Arizona Advocacy Network.

Had the court ruled otherwise, Wercinski said, it could have put at risk all other citizen-passed laws. He criticized the Republican-dominated Legislature for filing the challenge in the first place.

"I think it's unfortunate that every year we see a Republican majority backed by big-money special interests challenging laws that have been passed by the voters of Arizona," Wercinski said.

Proposition 106 was approved overwhelmingly by state voters in 2000. It created a five-member commission–two Democrats, two Republicans and one independent–that is charged with drawing congressional and legislative districts from scratch after every decennial Census.

Common Cause President Miles Rapoport said Monday's decision affirms Abraham Lincoln's declaration that "ours is a government of, by and for the people."

"Now that our highest court has given their initiative its blessing, we're hopeful that citizens and legislators alike in other states will push politics aside and create independent bodies to draw truly representative districts after the 2020 Census," Rapoport said.

Kathay Feng, national redistricting director for Common Cause, said the group will be working "across the country to end political gerrymandering through the creation of citizen-driven commissions like the one in Arizona."

Rep. Raul Grijalva, D-Tucson, said in a prepared statement that the court ruling validates the demands of Arizonans to leave partisan politics behind when it comes to drawing district boundaries.

"Elections are not games for politicians to rig, and this court decision makes clear that public officials cannot trump the will of the people in an attempt to stack the electoral map in their favor," his statement said.

1. Arizona legislators believe that they should have the right to redraw districts and that the Constitution protects those rights. Based on what you've learned, do you agree with them? Use examples from other cases in the book to make your argument.

2. In Arizona, citizens were allowed to vote on the redistricting panel. Do you think that such a move—letting voters have more control over their own redistricting—will help or hurt the problem of gerrymandering?

"FORMER AG HOLDER BLASTS GEORGIA REDISTRICTING 'POWER GRAB,'" FROM *SAJJA NEWS*, MARCH 15, 2017

Former U.S. Attorney General Eric Holder is hammering Georgia Republicans for what he calls a "power grab" as the GOP tries to redraw several legislative districts to benefit sitting lawmakers.

It's the first time Holder has weighed in on a state redistricting fight since he launched a national political organization intended to help Democrats in upcoming redistricting battles.

In a statement to The Associated Press, Holder says Republicans who control the Georgia House are practicing "political map-rigging at its worst" with a plan to move black voters out of certain swing districts in metro Atlanta.

"Voters should choose their elected representatives, not the other way around," Holder said of the proposal, which House Republicans adopted earlier this month on a party line vote.

The new district boundaries, which are now pending in the state Senate, would make it harder for Democratic challengers to defeat Republican incumbents.

Holder urged Republican Gov. Nathan Deal and GOP senators to reject the map.

The Georgia wrangle and Holder's response preview the former attorney general's strategy ahead of the 2020 census and subsequent legislative sessions where state lawmakers will redraw district boundaries that heavily influence the partisan makeup of Congress and state assemblies.

Georgia's General Assembly has state constitutional authority to redraw district boundaries "as necessary," though it's typically done after each decennial census, not late in a decade as Republicans are attempting now.

A spokeswoman for Deal said the governor does not comment on pending legislation.

The chairman of the state Senate's redistricting panel pointed to the longstanding tradition that each chamber allows the other to draw its own maps without interference; that effectively renders any upcoming Senate votes a formality.

"We don't alter theirs, and they don't alter ours," said Savannah Republican Ben Watson, who added that senators also are considering changes to their districts.

Nationally, Republicans were tremendously successful in the 2010 midterm elections, consolidating power in statehouses across the country. GOP majorities used that power to redraw congressional and legislative maps that in many states maximized the influence of conservative voters.

Essentially, the idea for a legislative majority is to concentrate opposition voters in as few districts as possible. The pending Georgia changes, for example, would move some heavily African-American precincts from GOP-held districts and into a district already occupied by a Democrat. Black voters overwhelmingly support Democrats.

The affected Republican incumbents have watched their winning margins drop as low as 51 and 53 percent in recent elections, so the GOP plan offers them insurance by shifting Democratic voters out of their districts.

Georgia House Speaker David Ralston defends the plan, saying it doesn't hurt any incumbent lawmaker, including the lone affected Democrat.

Those kinds of maneuvers, panned by critics as partisan and racial gerrymandering, help explain how a state like North Carolina is a presidential battleground with a Democratic governor, yet has a U.S. House delegation of 10 Republicans and three Democrats and a state

Legislature where the GOP began the year with a 74-46 majority in the House and a 35-15 majority in the Senate.

In Georgia, President Donald Trump won the state by 5 percentage points, while Deal won 2014 re-election by 8 points. But the U.S. House delegation is tilted 9-4 to the GOP, with one vacancy, while the GOP started the current year with a 118-62 majority in the state House and a 38-18 advantage in the state Senate.

There are several pending federal lawsuits challenging district boundaries around the country, including in North Carolina. A federal court ruled Friday that Texas lawmakers drew racially gerrymandered congressional districts in ways that minimize minority voter power.

Democrats also draw districts to their advantage, and activists in some states, separate from Holder's effort, are calling for bipartisan and independent commissions to take over redistricting power from partisan legislatures.

Georgia Republicans note that Democrats in the state, before they lost much of their power in 2002, drew district maps that courts ultimately threw out.

Now that it's Georgia Republicans redrawing lines, the input from a high-profile Democrat like Holder is unlikely to hold much sway. But Holder describes his overall effort as necessary to protect voting rights and the integrity of the political system.

His nascent group is the National Democratic Redistricting Committee, which he will use to advocate for what Democrats describe as fairer district boundaries. Former President Barack Obama is raising money for the organization.

1. Former US attorney general Eric Holder says that "voters should choose their elected representatives, not the other way around." Explain what he means by this.

2. In the article, Holder implies that sitting legislators in Georgia redrew the voting districts in order to benefit themselves and keep them in office. Explain why this is a problem. Do you think that legislators should have this right, since they won their seats through a democratic election? Or is their selective redistricting hurting democracy?

"'VICTORY FOR DEMOCRACY' AS COURT RULES AGAINST NORTH CAROLINA GERRYMANDERING," BY JAKE JOHNSON, FROM *COMMON DREAMS*, JANUARY 10, 2018

"PARTISAN GERRYMANDERS ARE QUITE SIMPLY UNDEMOCRATIC," DECLARED ONE OF THE ADVOCACY GROUPS LEADING THE LEGAL CHALLENGE AGAINST NORTH CAROLINA REPUBLICANS

[Editor's note: Links and PDFs can be found with the original article.]

In a ruling hailed as a major and historic "victory for democracy," a federal court on Tuesday deemed North Carolina's 2016 congressional map unconstitutional on the grounds that it was drawn to discriminate against Democratic voters—marking the first time a federal court has struck down a redistricting plan for partisan gerrymandering.

"Every American deserves representation in Washington, but the gerrymandered map struck down by the court today robbed much of the state of a representative voice in the nation's capital," said Karen Hobert Flynn, president of Common Cause, one of the advocacy groups the legal challenge against North Carolina's Republican Party. "Partisan gerrymanders are quite simply undemocratic."

The three-judge panel's decision (pdf) on Tuesday may have been unique in its stand against extreme partisan redistricting, but it was not the first time North Carolina's Republican-drawn congressional map has been struck down for violating the constitutional rights of voters. As Prema Levy of *Mother Jones* points out, "the state's previous map was deemed illegal for being racially gerrymandered in 2016"—years after the map allowed the GOP to take a vast majority of the state's House seats.

Following the 2016 ruling, North Carolina Republicans explicitly looked to structure the state's congressional map to give themselves a "partisan advantage"—resulting in what the Brennan Center for Justice called "one of the worst partisan gerrymanders of the decade."

"I acknowledge freely that this would be a political gerrymander, which is not against the law," Rep. David Lewis (R-N.C.), chairman of the state House's Redistricting Committee, declared during a 2016 meeting. "I think electing Republicans is better than electing Democrats. So I drew this map to help foster what I think is better for the country."

The North Carolina district court's determination on Tuesday that extreme partisan gerrymandering is, in fact, unconstitutional—violating the Equal Protection Clause, the First Amendment, and the Election Clause of Article I of the Constitution—is likely to gain national significance in the coming months, as the Supreme Court is currently considering two similar partisan gerrymandering cases in Wisconsin and Maryland.

North Carolina Republicans are expected to appeal to the Supreme Court to put the ruling on hold until the other two cases are decided—a delay that would allow the current map to remain in place through the 2018 midterm elections.

J. Michael Bitzer, professor of political science at Catawba College, told the *New York Times* that if Tuesday's ruling is upheld, it "gives hope to Democrats" looking to wrest control of the state's legislature from the GOP.

"I can imagine the Republicans being furious, but they have to see political reality, and it's not just in the next two weeks: It's come November," Bitzer concluded.

1. A politician in the article notes that since partisan gerrymandering is not illegal, and since he believes Republicans should be elected over Democrats, he drew a redistricting map that would support Republican candidates. Do you think that what he did was okay? Using evidence from other articles to support your argument, explain your reasoning.

2. In the past, racial gerrymandering has been deemed illegal. Why do you think one type of gerrymandering (partisan) is more acceptable than another (racial) to the people who make

the laws? Do you think racial and partisan gerrymandering should be considered different enough to be guided by different rules? Why or why not?

"ACHTUNG! VOTER SUPPRESSION IS COMING TO EUROPE," BY ANDREA SANDBRINK, FROM HEINRICH-BÖLL-STIFTUNG, NOVEMBER 2017

VOTER SUPPRESSION IS AT THE FOREFRONT OF THE US NATIONAL DEBATE. ARE THESE TACTICS NOW MAKING THEIR WAY TO EUROPE?

"I consider everything under 10% for AfD to be voter fraud" —AfD supporter on social media

"I would have won the popular vote if you deduct the millions of people that voted illegally" —US President Donald Trump

With an upcoming Supreme Court decision on partisan gerrymandering, new voter ID laws around the country, and increased rhetoric about voter fraud, the topic of voter suppression is at the forefront of the US national debate. For nearly 150 years, white legislators seeking to preserve their privilege and power have used these tactics to keep low-income and minority citizens from exercising their right to vote.

But while the United States is a pioneer in the field, it is not alone in struggling with the issues of voter suppression. Far-right, nationalist movements are spurring a rise in voter suppression tactics and fear-mongering about voter fraud in Europe, as well.

Voter ID laws are a favorite tactic by right-wing actors in the US, where the lack of a national ID means that it is disproportionately low-income and minority voters who do not have other forms of identification, like a driver's license or passport. In the United Kingdom, the Conservatives have been pushing for similar voter ID laws, even though only 0.00025 percent of votes cast in 2015 are alleged voter fraud cases. Northern Ireland is currently the only province in the UK in which voters have to show photo IDs. But in the 2018 elections, the Conservative Constitution Minister Chris Skidmore is implementing a pilot scheme in which five areas in England will serve as a trial for the rest of the country by requiring some form of identification to vote. Unlike in Northern Ireland, where the government provided free photo IDs when the new rules took effect, there are no plans to introduce a free card in the rest of the UK. According to the Electoral Commission, an estimated 3.5 million people do not have a photo ID and could lose their access to the voting process.

The UK is also experimenting with American-style partisan gerrymandering. A new proposal of electoral maps first introduced under former Conservative Prime Minister David Cameron designs the number of seats for an area not by how many people live there but by how many people were on the electoral register in December 2015. This would mean that the 2.5 million people that registered for the EU referendum would not be counted in the formation of new electoral districts. As it stands after the June 2016 election, the leftist Labour Party already needs more votes (40,290) to win one seat in UK Parliament than the Conservatives (a mere 34,244). The proposed changes would exacerbate this disparity. In addition, a new registration system that transitioned the voter registration process from a household registration to individual electoral registration purged around 800,000 people, mostly students, off its list when it was newly implemented amidst fear of voter fraud.

In Germany, where national elections were held on September 24, voter suppression tactics are not yet widespread. However, for the first time in Germany's history, the election saw heated rhetoric around voter fraud that resembled the US debate: The hashtag *#Wahlbetrug* (#voterfraud) trended on Twitter the day before the general elections, thanks to supporters of the right-wing party Alternative for Germany (AfD) and Russian Twitter bots. The AfD also called on its supporters to watch the vote count, suggesting that election workers might discount or invalidate some of their votes. The claim led the Organization for Security and Cooperation in Europe (OSCE) to send election observers to watch the vote count, a huge win for the AfD. Unlike Trump and Republicans in the US, the AfD, which holds only 12.6 percent of seats in parliament, is in no position to change voting laws or call a presidential commission. But its fear-mongering rhetoric has had a similar effect in sowing distrust and undermining the legitimacy of the democratic system.

In France, supporters of right-wing populist presidential candidate Marine Le Pen also made claims of voter fraud. They circulated accusations that Le Pen's opponents purposefully and systematically tore up ballots for the Front National candidate, and claimed that French citizens living abroad had voted twice. The claims were tinged with clear tones of anti-Semitism: "The Jewish community... arranged to have Le Pen's ballots destroyed," a right-wing online blog wrote following the election.

The voter suppression tactics that are beginning to appear in the UK, Germany, and France do not compare to the well-developed systems of disenfranchisement in the US. There, decades of voter suppression tactics have culminated in the new Presidential Advisory Commission on Election Integrity set up by the President. Trump has repeatedly said that his loss in the general election was due to 3 to 5 million people voting illegally, a statement that has no foundation in fact. The computer program that the Commission wants to implement nation-wide, the Interstate Crosscheck System, is meant to remove double registrations from voting lists but creates false positives 99 percent of the time. These can then be used to purge voters off voter registration lists. The vice chair and de facto head of the commission, Kris Kobach, was recently fined $1,000 for attempting to hide a document in which he advised the president on how to suppress the vote more effectively, revealing the true purpose of the commission once again.

If the US experience is any indication, the right-ward shift of established conservative parties and the rise of new right-wing political parties like the AfD and the Front National will likely spur an increase in voter suppression tactics. There is a real and significant risk that such trends will fundamentally undermine the public's trust in democratic institutions and processes, and allow an increasingly small number of people to hold disproportionate power.

1. Former UK prime minister David Cameron designed a system that would redraw voting districts based not on numbers of people who live there, but on registered voters who live there, which is being compared to the American style of gerrymandering. Do you think Cameron's plan constitutes gerrymandering? Explain.

CHAPTER 3

WHAT THE COURTS SAY

In the United States, the courts have had a hard time making a final determination on gerrymandering. From low-level local courts all the way up to the United States Supreme Court, it's been difficult for the judicial system to determine if gerrymandering is a real problem, and if it is a problem, how much of one it might be. But many cases have been heard—and some overturned—in the past several decades. As you read each one, you'll discover new evidence to support different views and will see how complicated the issue is when solid evidence is required to make a determination of gerrymandering.

EXCERPT FROM *DAVIS V. BANDEMER*, 478 U.S. 109 (1986), FROM THE US SUPREME COURT, JUNE 30, 1986

APPEAL FROM THE UNITED STATES DISTRICT COURT FOR THE SOUTHERN DISTRICT OF INDIANA

SYLLABUS

The Indiana Legislature consists of a 100-member House of Representatives and a 50-member Senate. Representatives serve 2-year terms, with elections for all seats every two years. Senators serve 4-year terms, with half of the seats up for election every two years. Senators are elected from single-member districts, while representatives are elected from a mixture of single-member and multimember districts. In 1981, the legislature reapportioned the districts pursuant to the 1980 census. At that time, there were Republican majorities in both the House and the Senate. The reapportionment plan provided 50 single-member districts for the Senate and 7 triple-member, 9 double-member, and 61 single-member districts for the House. The multimember districts generally included the State's metropolitan areas. In 1982, appellee Indiana Democrats filed suit in Federal District Court against appellant state officials, alleging that the 1981 reapportionment plan constituted a political gerrymander intended to disadvantage Democrats, and that the particular district lines that were drawn and the mix of single-member and multimember districts were intended to and did violate their right, as Democrats, to equal protection under the Fourteenth Amendment. In November 1982, before the case went to trial, elections were held under the new plan. Democratic candidates for the House received 51.9% of votes cast statewide, but only 43 out of the 100 seats to be filled. Democratic candidates for the Senate received 53.1% of the votes cast statewide, and 13 out of the 25 Democratic candidates were elected. In Marion and Allen Counties, both divided into multimember House districts, Democratic candidates drew 46.6% of the vote, but only 3 of the 21 Democratic candidates were elected. Subsequently, relying primarily on the 1982 election results as proof of unconstitutionally discriminatory vote dilution, the District Court invalidated the 1981 reapportionment plan, enjoined appellants from holding elections pursuant thereto, and ordered the legislature to prepare a new plan.

Held: The judgment is reversed. [...]

JUSTICE WHITE delivered the opinion of the Court with respect to Part II, concluding that political gerrymandering, such as occurred in this case, is properly justiciable under the Equal Protection Clause. Pp. 478 U. S. 127-143.

Here, none of the identifying characteristics of a nonjusticiable political question are present. Disposition of the case does not involve this Court in a matter more properly decided by a coequal branch of the Government. There is no risk of foreign or domestic disturbance. Nor is this Court persuaded that there are no judicially discernible and manageable standards by which political gerrymandering cases are to be decided. The mere fact that there is no likely arithmetic presumption, such as the "one person, one vote" rule, in the present context does not compel a conclusion that the claims presented here are nonjusticiable. The claim is whether each political group in the State should have the same chance to elect representatives of its choice as any other political group, and this Court declines to hold that such claim is never justiciable. That the claim is submitted by a political group, rather than a racial group, does not distinguish it in terms of justiciability. Pp. 478 U. S. 118-127.

JUSTICE WHITE, joined by JUSTICE BRENNAN, JUSTICE MARSHALL, and JUSTICE BLACKMUN, concluded in Parts III and IV that the District Court erred in holding that appellees had alleged and proved a violation of the Equal Protection Clause. Pp. 478 U. S. 127-143.

(a) A threshold showing of discriminatory vote dilution is required for a *prima facie* case of an equal protection violation. The District Court's findings of an adverse effect on appellees do not surmount this threshold requirement. The mere fact that an apportionment scheme makes it more difficult for a particular group in a particular district to elect representatives of its choice does not render that scheme unconstitutional. A group's electoral power is not unconstitutionally diminished by the fact that an apportionment scheme makes winning elections more difficult, and a failure of proportional representation alone does not constitute impermissible discrimination under the Equal Protection Clause. As with individual districts, where unconstitutional vote dilution is alleged in the form of statewide political gerrymandering, as here, the mere lack of proportional representation will not be sufficient to prove unconstitutional discrimination. Without specific supporting evidence, a court cannot presume in such a case that those who are elected will disregard the disproportionally underrepresented group. Rather, unconstitutional discrimination occurs only when the electoral system is arranged in a manner that will consistently degrade a voter's or a group of voters' influence on the political process as a whole. The District Court's apparent holding that any interference with an opportunity to elect a representative of one's choice would be sufficient to allege or prove an equal protection violation, unless justified by some acceptable state interest, in addition to being contrary to the above-described conception of an unconstitutional political gerrymander, would invite attack on all or almost all reapportionment statutes. Pp. 478 U. S. 127-134.

(b) Relying on a single election to prove unconstitutional discrimination, as the District Court did, is unsatisfactory. Without finding that, because of the 1981 reapportionment, the Democrats could not in one of the next few elections secure a sufficient vote to take control of the legislature, that the reapportionment would consign the Democrats to a minority status in the legislature throughout the 1980's, or that they would have no hope of doing any better in the reapportionment based on the 1990 census, the District Court erred in concluding that the 1981 reapportionment violated the Equal

Protection Clause. Simply showing that there are multimember districts, and that those districts are constructed so as to be safely Republican or Democratic, in no way bolsters the contention that there has been a statewide discrimination against Democratic voters. Pp. 478 U. S. 134-137.

(c) The view that intentional drawing of district boundaries for partisan ends, and for no other reason, violates the Equal Protection Clause would allow a constitutional violation to be found where the only proven effect on a political party's electoral power was disproportionate results in one election (possibly two elections), and would invite judicial interference in legislative districting whenever a political party suffers at the polls. Even if a state legislature redistricts with the specific intention of disadvantaging one political party's election prospects, there has been no unconstitutional violation against members of that party unless the redistricting does, in fact, disadvantage it at the polls. As noted, a mere lack of proportionate results in one election cannot suffice in this regard. Pp. 478 U. S. 138-143.

JUSTICE O'CONNOR, joined by THE CHIEF JUSTICE and JUSTICE REHNQUIST, concluding that the partisan gerrymandering claims of major political parties raise a nonjusticiable political question, would reverse the District Court's judgment on the grounds that appellees' claim is nonjusticiable. The Equal Protection Clause does not supply judicially manageable standards for resolving purely political gerrymandering claims, and does not confer group rights to an equal share of political power.

Racial gerrymandering claims are justiciable because of the greater warrant the Equal Protection Clause gives the federal courts to intervene for protection against racial discrimination, and because of the stronger nexus between individual rights and group interests that is present in the case of a discrete and insular racial group. But members of the major political parties cannot claim that they are vulnerable to exclusion from the political process, and it has not been established that there is a need or a constitutional basis for judicial intervention to resolve political gerrymandering claims. The costs of judicial intervention will be severe, and such intervention requires courts to make policy choices that are not of a kind suited for judicial discretion. Nor is there any clear stopping point to prevent the gradual evolution of a requirement of roughly proportional representation for every cohesive political group. Accordingly, political gerrymandering claims present a nonjusticiable political question. Pp. 478 U. S. 144-155.

WHITE, J., announced the judgment of the Court and delivered the opinion of the Court with respect to Part II, in which BRENNAN, MARSHALL, BLACKMUN, POWELL, and STEVENS, JJ., joined, and an opinion with respect to Parts I, III, and IV, in which BRENNAN, MARSHALL, and BLACKMUN, JJ., joined. BURGER, C. J., filed an opinion concurring in the judgment, post, p. 478 U. S. 143. O'CONNOR, J., filed an opinion concurring in the judgment, in which BURGER, C. J., and REHNQUIST, J., joined. POWELL, J., filed an opinion concurring in part and dissenting in part, in which STEVENS, J., joined, post, p. 478 U. S. 161.

JUSTICE WHITE announced the judgment of the Court and delivered the opinion of the Court as to

Part II and an opinion as to Parts I, III, and IV, in which JUSTICE BRENNAN, JUSTICE MARSHALL, and JUSTICE BLACKMUN join.

In this case, we review a judgment from a three-judge District Court which sustained an equal protection challenge to Indiana's 1981 state apportionment on the basis that the law unconstitutionally diluted the votes of Indiana Democrats. 603 F.Supp. 1479 (SD Ind.1984). Although we find such political gerrymandering to be justiciable, we conclude that the District Court applied an insufficiently demanding standard in finding unconstitutional vote dilution. Consequently, we reverse.

I

The Indiana Legislature, also known as the "General Assembly," consists of a House of Representatives and a Senate. There are 100 members of the House of Representatives, and 50 members of the Senate. The members of the House serve 2-year terms, with elections held for all seats every two years. The members of the Senate serve 4-year terms, and Senate elections are staggered, so that half of the seats are up for election every two years. The members of both Houses are elected from legislative districts, but, while all Senate members are elected from single-member districts, House members are elected from a mixture of single-member and multimember districts. The division of the State into districts is accomplished by legislative enactment, which is signed by the Governor into law. Reapportionment is required every 10 years, and is based on the federal decennial census. There is no prohibition against more frequent reapportionments.

In early 1981, the General Assembly initiated the process of reapportioning the State's legislative districts pursuant to the 1980 census. At this time, there were Republican majorities in both the House and the Senate, and the Governor was Republican.[1] Bills were introduced in both Houses, and a reapportionment plan was duly passed and approved by the Governor.[2] This plan provided 50 single-member districts for the Senate; for the House, it provided 7 triple-member, 9 double-member, and 61 single-member districts. In the Senate plan, the population deviation between districts was 1.15%; in the House plan, the deviation was 1.05%. The multimember districts generally included the more metropolitan areas of the State, although not every metropolitan area was in a multimember district. Marion County, which includes Indianapolis, was combined with portions of its neighboring counties to form five triple-member districts. Fort Wayne was divided into two parts, and each part was combined with portions of the surrounding county or counties to make two triple-member districts. On the other hand, South Bend was divided and put partly into a double-member district and partly into a single-member district (each part combined with part of the surrounding county or counties). Although county and city lines were not consistently followed, township lines generally were. The two plans, the Senate and the House, were not nested -- that is, each Senate district was not divided exactly into two House districts. There appears to have been little relation between the lines drawn in the two plans.

In early 1982, this suit was filed by several Indiana Democrats (here the appellees) against various state officials (here the appellants), alleging that the

1981 reapportionment plans constituted a political gerrymander intended to disadvantage Democrats. Specifically, they contended that the particular district lines that were drawn and the mix of single-member and multimember districts were intended to, and did, violate their right, as Democrats, to equal protection under the Fourteenth Amendment. A three-judge District Court was convened to hear these claims.

In November, 1982, before the case went to trial, elections were held under the new districting plan. All of the House seats and half of the Senate seats were up for election. Over all the House races statewide, Democratic candidates received 51.9% of the vote. Only 43 Democrats, however, were elected to the House. Over all the Senate races statewide, Democratic candidates received 53.1% of the vote. Thirteen (of twenty-five) Democrats were elected. In Marion and Allen Counties, both divided into multimember House districts, Democratic candidates drew 46.6% of the vote, but only 3 of the 21 House seats were filled by Democrats.

On December 13, 1984, a divided District Court issued a decision declaring the reapportionment to be unconstitutional, enjoining the appellants from holding elections pursuant to the 1981 redistricting, ordering the General Assembly to prepare a new plan, and retaining jurisdiction over the case. See 603 F.Supp. 1479.

To the District Court majority, the results of the 1982 elections seemed "to support an argument that there is a built-in bias favoring the majority party, the Republicans, which instituted the reapportionment plan." Id. at 1486. Although the court thought that these figures were unreliable predictors of future elections, it concluded that they warranted further examination of the circumstances surrounding the passage of the reapportionment statute. *See ibid.*[3] In the course of this further examination, the court noted the irregular shape of some district lines, the peculiar mix of single-member and multimember districts,[4] and the failure of the district lines to adhere consistently to political subdivision boundaries to define communities of interest. The court also found inadequate the other explanations given for the configuration of the districts, such as adherence to the one person, one vote imperative and the Voting Rights Act's no-retrogression requirement. These factors, concluded the court, evidenced an intentional effort to favor Republican incumbents and candidates and to disadvantage Democratic voters.[5] This was achieved by "stacking" Democrats into districts with large Democratic majorities and "splitting" them in other districts, so as to give Republicans safe but not excessive majorities in those districts.[6] Because the 1982 elections indicated that the plan also had a discriminatory effect, in that the proportionate voting influence of Democratic voters had been adversely affected and because any scheme "which purposely inhibit[s] or prevent[s] proportional representation cannot be tolerated," *id.* at 1492, the District Court invalidated the statute.[7]

The defendants appealed, seeking review of the District Court's rulings that the case was justiciable and that, if justiciable, an equal protection violation had occurred.[8] We noted probable jurisdiction. 470 U.S. 1083 (1985).

II

We address first the question whether this case presents a justiciable controversy or a nonjusticiable political question. Although the District Court never explicitly stated that the case was justiciable, its holding clearly rests on such a finding. The appellees urge that this Court has in the past acknowledged and acted upon the justiciability of purely political gerrymandering claims. The appellants contend that we have affirmed on the merits decisions of lower courts finding such claims to be nonjusticiable.

A

Since *Baker v. Carr*, 369 U. S. 186 (1962), we have consistently adjudicated equal protection claims in the legislative districting context regarding inequalities in population between districts. In the course of these cases, we have developed and enforced the "one person, one vote" principle. *See, e.g., Reynolds v. Sims*, 377 U. S. 533 (1964).

Our past decisions also make clear that, even where there is no population deviation among the districts, racial gerrymandering presents a justiciable equal protection claim. In the multimember district context, we have reviewed, and on occasion rejected, districting plans that unconstitutionally diminished the effectiveness of the votes of racial minorities. See *Rogers v. Lodge*, 458 U. S. 613 (1982); *Mobile v. Bolden*, 446 U. S. 55 (1980); *White v. Regester*, 412 U. S. 755 (1973); *Whitcomb v. Chavis*, 403 U. S. 124 (1971); *Burns v. Richardson*, 384 U. S. 73 (1966); *Fortson v. Dorsey*, 379 U. S. 433 (1965). We have also adjudicated claims that the configuration of single-member districts violated equal protection with respect to racial and ethnic minorities, although we have never struck down an apportionment plan because of such a claim. *See United Jewish Organizations of Williamsburgh, Inc. v. Carey*, 430 U. S. 144 (1977); *Wright v. Rockefeller*, 376 U. S. 52 (1964).

In the multimember district cases, we have also repeatedly stated that districting that would "operate to minimize or cancel out the voting strength of racial or *political* elements of the voting population" would raise a constitutional question. *Fortson, supra*, at 439 (emphasis added). *See also Gaffney v. Cummings*, 412 U. S. 735, 412 U. S. 751 (1973); *Whitcomb v. Chavis, supra*, at 403 U. S. 143; *Burns v. Richardson, supra*, at 384 U. S. 88. Finally, in *Gaffney v. Cummings, supra*, we upheld against an equal protection political gerrymandering challenge a state legislative single-member redistricting scheme that was formulated in a bipartisan effort to try to provide political representation on a level approximately proportional to the strength of political parties in the State. In that case, we adjudicated the type of purely political equal protection claim that is brought here, although we did not, as a threshold matter, expressly hold such a claim to be justiciable. Regardless of this lack of a specific holding, our consideration of the merits of the claim in *Gaffney* in the face of a discussion of justiciability in appellant's brief, combined with our repeated reference in other opinions to the constitutional deficiencies of plans that dilute the vote of political groups, at the least supports an inference that these cases are justiciable.

In the years since *Baker v. Carr*, both before and after *Gaffney*, however, we have also affirmed a number

WHAT THE COURTS SAY

of decisions in which the lower courts rejected the justiciability of purely political gerrymandering claims. In *WMCA, Inc. v. Lomenzo*, 382 U. S. 4 (1965), *summarily aff'g* 238 F.Supp. 916 (SDNY), the most frequently cited of these cases, we affirmed the decision of a three-judge District Court upholding a temporary apportionment plan for the State of New York. The District Court had determined that political gerrymandering equal protection challenges to this plan were nonjusticiable. *See id.* at 925-926. Justice Harlan, in his opinion concurring in the Court's summary affirmance, expressed his understanding that the affirmance was based on the Court's approval of the lower court's finding of nonjusticiability. See 382 U.S. at 382 U. S. 6. *See also Jimenez v. Hidalgo County Water Improvement District* No. 2, 424 U.S. 950 (1976), *summarily aff'g* 68 F.R.D. 668 (SD Tex. 1975); *Ferrell v. Hall*, 406 U.S. 939 (1972), *summarily aff'g* 339 F.Supp. 73 (WD Okla.); *Wells v. Rockefeller*, 398 U.S. 901 (1970), *summarily aff'g* 311 F.Supp. 48 (SDNY). Although these summary affirmances arguably support an inference that these claims are not justiciable, there are other cases in which federal or state courts adjudicated political gerrymandering claims and we summarily affirmed or dismissed for want of a substantial federal question. *See, e.g., Wiser v. Hughes*, 459 U.S. 962 (1982), dismissing for want of a substantial federal question an appeal from *In re Legislative Districting*, 299 Md. 658, 475 A. 2d 428; *Kelly v. Bumpers*, 413 U.S. 901 (1973), *summarily aff'g* 340 F.Supp. 568 (ED Ark.1972); Archer v. Smith, 409 U.S. 808 (1972), *summarily aff'g Graves v. Barnes*, 343 F.Supp. 704, 734 (WD Tex.).

These sets of cases may look in different directions, but to the extent that our summary affirmances indicate the nonjusticiability of political gerrymander cases, we are not bound by those decisions. As we have observed before,

> "[i]t is not at all unusual for the Court to find it appropriate to give full consideration to a question that has been the subject of previous summary action."

Washington v. Yakima Indian Nation, 439 U. S. 463, 439 U. S. 477, n. 20 (1979). See also *Edelman v. Jordan*, 415 U. S. 651, 415 U. S. 670-671 (1974). The issue that the appellants would have us find to be precluded by these summary dispositions is an important one, and it deserves further consideration.

B

The outlines of the political question doctrine were described and to a large extent defined in *Baker v. Carr*. The synthesis of that effort is found in the following passage in the Court's opinion:

> "It is apparent that several formulations which vary slightly according to the settings in which the questions arise may describe a political question, although each has one or more elements which identify it as essentially a function of the separation of powers. Prominent on the surface of any case held to involve a political question is found a textually demonstrable constitutional commitment of the issue to a coordinate political department; or a lack of judicially discoverable and manageable standards for resolving it; or the impossibility of deciding without an initial policy determination of a kind clearly for nonjudicial

discretion; or the impossibility of a court's under-taking independent resolution without expressing lack of the respect due coordinate branches of government; or an unusual need for unques-tioning adherence to a political decision already made; or the potentiality of embarrassment from multifarious pronouncements by various depart-ments on one question. "

"Unless one of these formulations is inextricable from the case at bar, there should be no dismissal for nonjusticiability on the ground of a political question's presence. The doctrine of which we treat is one of 'political questions,' not one of 'polit-ical cases.' The courts cannot reject as 'no law suit' a bona fide controversy as to whether some action denominated 'political' exceeds consti-tutional authority. The cases we have reviewed show the necessity for discriminating inquiry into the precise facts and posture of the particular case, and the impossibility of resolution by any semantic cataloguing."

369 U.S. at 369 U. S. 217.

In *Baker*, the Court applied this analysis to an equal protection claim based on a state legislative apportionment that allowed substantial disparities in the number of voters represented by each state representative. *See id.* at 369 U. S. 253-258 (Clark, J., concurring). In holding that claim to be justiciable, the Court concluded that none of the identi-fying characteristics of a political question were present:

"The question here is the consistency of state action with the Federal Constitution. We have no question decided, or to be decided, by a political branch of government coequal with this Court. Nor do we risk embarrassment of our government abroad, or grave disturbance at home if we take issue with Tennessee as to the constitutionality of her action here challenged. Nor need the appellants, in order to succeed in this action, ask the Court to enter upon policy determinations for which judicially manageable standards are lacking. Judicial standards under the Equal Protection Clause are well developed and familiar, and it has been open to courts since the enactment of the Fourteenth Amendment to determine, if on the particular facts they must, that a discrimination reflects no policy, but simply arbitrary and capricious action."

Id. at 369 U. S. 226.

This analysis applies equally to the question now before us. Disposition of this question does not involve us in a matter more properly decided by a coequal branch of our Government. There is no risk of foreign or domestic disturbance, and, in light of our cases since *Baker*, we are not persuaded that there are no judicially discernible and manageable standards by which political gerrymander cases are to be decided.

It is true that the type of claim that was presented in *Baker v. Carr* was subsequently resolved in this Court by the formulation of the "one person, one vote" rule. *See, e.g., Reynolds v. Sims*, 377 U.S. at 377 U. S. 557-561. The mere fact, however, that we may not now similarly perceive a likely arithmetic presumption in the instant context does not compel a conclusion that the claims presented here are nonjusticiable. The one person, one vote principle had not yet been developed when Baker was decided. At that time, the Court did not rely on the potential for such a rule in finding justiciability. Instead, as the language quoted above clearly indicates, the Court contemplated simply that legislative linedrawing in the districting context would be susceptible of adjudication under the applicable constitutional criteria.

Furthermore, in formulating the one person, one vote formula, the Court characterized the question posed by election districts of disparate size as an issue of fair representation. In such cases, it is not that anyone is deprived of a vote or that any person's vote is not counted. Rather, it is that one electoral district elects a single representative and another district of the same size elects two or more -- the elector's vote in the former district having less weight in the sense that he may vote for and his district be represented by only one legislator, while his neighbor in the adjoining district votes for and is represented by two or more. *Reynolds* accordingly observed:

> "Since the achieving of fair and effective representation for all citizens is concededly the basic aim of legislative apportionment, we conclude that the Equal Protection Clause guarantees the opportunity for equal participation by all voters in the election of State legislators. Diluting the weight of votes because of place of residence impairs basic constitutional rights under the Fourteenth Amendment just as much as invidious discriminations based upon factors such as race. . . ."

377 U.S. at 377 U. S. 565-566. *Reynolds* surely indicates the justiciability of claims going to the adequacy of representation in state legislatures.

The issue here is, of course, different from that adjudicated in *Reynolds*. It does not concern districts of unequal size. Not only does everyone have the right to vote and to have his vote counted, but each elector may vote for and be represented by the same number of lawmakers. Rather, the claim is that each political group in a State should have the same chance to elect representatives of its choice as any other political group. Nevertheless, the issue is one of representation, and we decline to hold that such claims are never justiciable.

Our racial gerrymander cases such as *White v. Regester* and *Whitcomb v. Chavis* indicate as much. In those cases, there was no population variation among the districts, and no one was precluded from voting. The claim instead was that an identifiable racial or ethnic group had an insufficient chance to elect a representative of its choice, and that district lines should be redrawn to remedy this alleged defect. In both cases, we adjudicated the merits of such claims, rejecting the claim in *Whitcomb* and sustaining it in *Regester*. Just as clearly, in *Gaffney v. Cummings*, where the districts also passed muster under the *Reynolds* formula, the claim was that the legislature had manipulated district lines to afford political groups in various districts an enhanced opportunity to elect legislators of their choice. Although advising caution, we said that

> "we *must* . . . respond to [the] claims . . . that, even if acceptable population-wise, the . . . plan was invidiously discriminatory because a 'political fairness principle' was followed. . . ."

412 U.S. at 412 U. S. 751-752 (emphasis added). We went on to hold that the statute at issue did not violate the Equal Protection Clause.

These decisions support a conclusion that this case is justiciable. As *Gaffney* demonstrates, that the claim is submitted by a political group, rather than a racial group, does not distinguish it in terms of justiciability. That the characteristics of the complaining group are not immutable, or that the group has not been subject to the same historical stigma, may be relevant to the manner in which the case is adjudicated, but these differences do not justify a refusal to entertain such a case.

In fact, JUSTICE O'CONNOR's attempt to distinguish this political gerrymandering claim from the racial gerry-mandering claims that we have consistently adjudicated demonstrates the futility of such an effort. Her conclusion that the claim in this case is not justiciable seems to rest on a dual concern that no judicially manageable stan-dards exist, and that adjudication of such claims requires an initial policy decision that the judiciary should not make. Yet she does not point out how the standards that we set forth here for adjudicating this political gerryman-dering claim are less manageable than the standards that have been developed for racial gerrymandering claims. Nor does she demonstrate what initial policy decision -- regarding, for example, the desirability of fair group repre-sentation -- we have made here that we have not made in the race cases.[9] She merely asserts that, because race has historically been a suspect classification, individual minority voters' rights are more immediately related to a racial minority group's voting strength. This, in combi-nation with "the greater warrant the Equal Protection Clause gives the federal courts to intervene for protec-tion against racial discrimination, suffice to render racial gerrymandering claims justiciable." *Post* at 478 U. S. 151 (O'CONNOR, J., concurring in judgment).

Reliance on these assertions to determine justiciability would transform the narrow categories of "political
questions" that *Baker v. Carr* carefully defined into an ad
hoc litmus test of this Court's reactions to the desirability
of, and need for, judicial application of constitutional or
statutory standards to a given type of claim. JUSTICE
O'CONNOR's own discussion seems to reflect such an
approach: she concludes that, because political gerrymandering may be a "self-limiting enterprise" there is
no need for judicial intervention. *Post* at 478 U. S. 152.
She also expresses concern that our decision today will
lead to "political instability and judicial malaise," post at
478 U. S. 147, because nothing will prevent members of
other identifiable groups from bringing similar claims. To
begin with, JUSTICE O'CONNOR's factual assumptions
are by no means obviously correct: it is not clear that
political gerrymandering is a self-limiting enterprise, or
that other groups will have any great incentive to bring
gerrymandering claims, given the requirement of a
showing of discriminatory intent. At a more fundamental
level, however, JUSTICE O'CONNOR's analysis is flawed
because it focuses on the perceived need for judicial
review and on the potential practical problems with
allowing such review. Validation of the consideration of
such amorphous and wide-ranging factors in assessing
justiciability would alter substantially the analysis
the Court enunciated in *Baker v. Carr*, and we decline
JUSTICE O'CONNOR's implicit invitation to rethink that
approach.
[...]

IV

In sum, we hold that political gerrymandering cases are properly justiciable under the Equal Protection Clause. We also conclude, however, that a threshold showing of discriminatory vote dilution is required for a prima facie case of an equal protection violation. In this case, the findings made by the District Court of an adverse effect on the appellees do not surmount the threshold requirement. Consequently, the judgment of the District Court is
Reversed.

1. The justices argue that proving partisan gerrymandering and its negative effects on the electorate is difficult. Based on the evidence presented in this case, do you agree with their ruling?

2. Other, more recent Supreme Court cases on gerrymandering are discussed in this chapter. Based on what you've read about this case and the others, how has the issue changed since the Supreme Court's 1986 decision? Do you think there is enough evidence for the court to make a different ruling today?

RUTH O. SHAW, ET AL., APPELLANTS V. JANET RENO, ATTORNEY GENERAL, ET AL., FROM THE US SUPREME COURT, JUNE 28, 1993

ON APPEAL FROM THE UNITED STATES DISTRICT COURT FOR THE EASTERN DISTRICT OF NORTH CAROLINA

Justice O'Connor delivered the opinion of the Court.

The voting age population of North Carolina is approximately 78% white, 20% black, and 1% Native American; the remaining 1% is predominantly Asian. App. to Brief for Federal Appellees 16a. The black population is relatively dispersed; blacks constitute a majority of the general population in only 5 of the State's 100 counties. Brief for Appellants 57. Geographically, the State divides into three regions: the eastern Coastal Plain, the central Piedmont Plateau, and the western mountains. H. Lefler & A. Newsom, The History of a Southern State: North Carolina 18-22 (3d ed. 1973). The largest concentrations of black citizens live in the Coastal Plain, primarily in the northern part. O. Gade & H. Stillwell, North Carolina: People and Environments 65-68 (1986). The General Assembly's first redistricting plan contained one majority-black district centered in that area of the State.

Forty of North Carolina's one hundred counties are covered by § 5 of the Voting Rights Act of 1965, 42 U. S. C. § 1973c, which prohibits a jurisdiction subject to its provisions from implementing changes in a "standard, practice, or procedure with respect to voting" without federal authorization, ibid. The jurisdiction must obtain either a judgment from the United States District Court for the District of Columbia declaring that the proposed change "does not have the purpose and will not have the effect of denying or abridging the right to vote on account of race or color" or administrative preclearance from the Attorney General. *Ibid.* Because the General Assembly's reapportionment plan affected the covered counties, the parties agree that § 5 applied. Tr. of Oral Arg. 14, 27-29. The State chose to submit its plan to the Attorney General for preclearance.

The Attorney General, acting through the Assistant Attorney General for the Civil Rights Division, interposed a formal objection to the General Assembly's plan. The Attorney General specifically objected to the config-uration of boundary lines drawn in the south-central to southeastern region of the State. In the Attorney General's view, the General Assembly could have created a second majority-minority district "to give effect to black and Native American voting strength in this area" by using boundary lines "no more irregular than [those] found elsewhere in the proposed plan," but failed to do so for "pretextual reasons." See App. to Brief for Federal Appellees l0a-l1a.

Under § 5, the State remained free to seek a declaratory judgment from the District Court for the District of Columbia notwithstanding the Attorney General's objection. It did not do so. Instead, the General Assembly enacted a revised redistricting plan, 1991 N. C. Extra Sess. Laws, ch. 7, that included a second majority-black district. The General Assembly located the second district not in the south-central to southeastern part of the State, but in the north-central region along Interstate 85. See Appendix.

The first of the two majority-black districts contained in the revised plan, District 1, is somewhat hook shaped. Centered in the northeast portion of the State, it moves southward until it tapers to a narrow band; then, with finger-like extensions, it reaches far into the southernmost part of the State near the South Carolina border. District 1 has been compared to a "Rorschach ink-blot test," *Shaw v. Barr*, 808 F. Supp. 461, 476 (EDNC 1992) (Voorhees, C. J., concurring in part and dissenting in part), and a "bug splattered on a windshield," Wall Street Journal, Feb. 4, 1992, p. A14.

The second majority-black district, District 12, is even more unusually shaped. It is approximately 160 miles long and, for much of its length, no wider than the 1-85 corridor. It winds in snakelike fashion through tobacco country, financial centers, and manufacturing areas "until it gobbles in enough enclaves of black neighborhoods." 808 F. Supp., at 476-477 (Voorhees, C. J., concurring in part and dissenting in part). Northbound and southbound drivers on 1-85 sometimes find themselves in separate districts in one county, only to "trade" districts when they enter the next county. Of the 10 counties through which District 12 passes, 5 are cut into 3 different districts; even towns are divided. At one point the district remains contiguous only because it intersects at a single point with two other districts before crossing over them. See Brief for Republican National Committee as Amicus Curiae 14-15. One state legislator has remarked that" '[i]f you drove down the interstate with both car doors open, you'd kill most of the people in the district.'" Washington Post, Apr. 20, 1993, p. A4. The district even has inspired poetry: "Ask not for whom the line is drawn; it is drawn to avoid thee." Grofman, Would Vince Lombardi Have Been Right If He Had Said: "When It Comes to Redistricting, Race Isn't Everything, It's the Only Thing"?, 14 Cardozo L. Rev. 1237, 1261, n. 96 (1993) (internal quotation marks omitted).

The Attorney General did not object to the General Assembly's revised plan. But numerous North Carolinians did. The North Carolina Republican Party and individual voters brought suit in Federal District Court, alleging that the plan constituted an unconstitutional political gerrymander under *Davis v. Bandemer*, 478 U. S. 109 (1986). That claim was dismissed, see *Pope v. Blue*, 809 F. Supp. 392 (WDNC), and this Court summarily affirmed, 506 U. S. 801 (1992).

Shortly after the complaint in Pope v. Blue was filed, appellants instituted the present action in the United States District Court for the Eastern District of North Carolina. Appellants alleged not that the revised plan constituted a political gerrymander, nor that it violated the "one person, one vote" principle, see *Reynolds v. Sims*, 377 U. S. 533, 558 (1964), but that the State had created an unconstitutional racial gerrymander. Appellants are five residents of Durham County, North Carolina, all registered to vote in that county. Under the General Assembly's plan, two will vote for congressional representatives in District 12 and three will vote in neighboring District 2. Appellants sued the Governor of North Carolina, the Lieutenant Governor, the Secretary of State, the Speaker of the North Carolina House of Representatives, and members of the North Carolina State Board of Elections (state appellees), together with two federal officials, the Attorney General and the Assistant Attorney General for the Civil Rights Division (federal appellees).

Appellants contended that the General Assembly's revised reapportionment plan violated several provisions of the United States Constitution, including the Fourteenth Amendment. They alleged that the General Assembly deliberately "create[d] two Congressional Districts in which a majority of black voters was concentrated arbitrarily—without regard to any other considerations, such as compactness, contiguousness, geographical boundaries, or political subdivisions" with the purpose "to create Congressional Districts along racial lines" and to assure the election of two black representatives to Congress. App. to Juris. Statement 102a. Appellants sought declaratory and injunctive relief against the state appellees. They sought similar relief against the federal appellees, arguing, alternatively, that the federal appellees had misconstrued the Voting Rights Act or that the Act itself was unconstitutional.

The three-judge District Court granted the federal appellees' motion to dismiss. 808 F. Supp. 461 (EDNC 1992). The court agreed unanimously that it lacked subject matter jurisdiction by reason of § 14(b) of the Voting Rights Act, 42 U. S. C. § 1973l(b), which vests the District Court for the District of Columbia with exclusive jurisdiction to issue injunctions against the execution of the Act and to enjoin actions taken by federal officers pursuant thereto. 808 F. Supp., at 466-467; *id.*, at 474 (Voorhees, C. J., concurring in relevant part). Two judges also concluded that, to the extent appellants challenged the Attorney General's preclearance decisions, their claim was foreclosed by this Court's holding in *Morris v. Gressette*, 432 U. S. 491 (1977). 808 F. Supp., at 467.

By a 2-to-1 vote, the District Court also dismissed the complaint against the state appellees. The majority found no support for appellants' contentions that race-based districting is prohibited by Article I, § 4, or Article I, § 2, of the Constitution, or by the Privileges and Immunities Clause of the Fourteenth Amendment. It deemed appellants' claim under the Fifteenth Amendment essentially subsumed within their related claim under the Equal Protection Clause. 808 F. Supp., at 468-469. That claim, the majority concluded, was barred by *United Jewish Organizations of Williamsburgh, Inc. v. Carey*, 430 U. S. 144 (1977) (*UJO*).

The majority first took judicial notice of a fact omitted from appellants' complaint: that appellants are white. It rejected the argument that race-conscious redistricting to benefit minority voters is per se unconstitutional. The majority also rejected appellants' claim that North Carolina's reapportionment plan was impermissible. The majority read *UJO* to stand for the proposition that a redistricting scheme violates white voters' rights only if it is "adopted with the purpose and effect of discriminating against white voters ... on account of their race." 808 F. Supp., at 472. The purposes of favoring minority voters and complying with the Voting Rights Act are not discriminatory in the constitutional sense, the court reasoned, and majority-minority districts have an impermissibly discriminatory effect only when they unfairly dilute or cancel out white voting strength. Because the State's purpose here was to comply with the Voting Rights Act, and because the General Assembly's plan did not lead to proportional

CRITICAL PERSPECTIVES ON GERRYMANDERING

underrepresentation of white voters statewide, the majority concluded that appellants had failed to state an equal protection claim. *Id.*, at 472-473.

Chief Judge Voorhees agreed that race-conscious redistricting is not per se unconstitutional but dissented from the rest of the majority's equal protection analysis. He read Justice White's opinion in *UJO* to authorize race-based reapportionment only when the State employs traditional districting principles such as compactness and contiguity. 808 F. Supp., at 475-477 (opinion concurring in part and dissenting in part). North Carolina's failure to respect these principles, in Judge Voorhees' view, "augur[ed] a constitutionally suspect, and potentially unlawful, intent" sufficient to defeat the state appellees' motion to dismiss. Id., at 477.

We noted probable jurisdiction. 506 U. S. 1019 (19920.

"The right to vote freely for the candidate of one's choice is of the essence of a democratic society .... " *Reynolds v. Sims*, 377 U. S., at 555. For much of our Nation's history, that right sadly has been denied to many because of race. The Fifteenth Amendment, ratified in 1870 after a bloody Civil War, promised unequivocally that "[t]he right of citizens of the United States to vote" no longer would be "denied or abridged ... by any State on account of race, color, or previous condition of servitude." U. S. Const., Amdt. 15, § 1.

But "[a] number of states ... refused to take no for an answer and continued to circumvent the fifteenth amendment's prohibition through the use of both subtle and blunt instruments, perpetuating ugly patterns of pervasive racial discrimination." Blumstein, Defining and Proving Race Discrimination: Perspectives on the

Purpose V s. Results Approach from the Voting Rights Act, 69 Va. L. Rev. 633, 637 (1983). Ostensibly race-neutral devices such as literacy tests with "grandfather" clauses and "good character" provisos were devised to deprive black voters of the franchise. Another of the weapons in the States' arsenal was the racial gerrymander—"the deliberate and arbitrary distortion of district boundaries ... for [racial] purposes." *Bandemer*, 478 U. S., at 164 (Powell, J., concurring in part and dissenting in part) (internal quotation marks omitted). In the 1870's, for example, opponents of Reconstruction in Mississippi "concentrated the bulk of the black population in a 'shoestring' Congressional district running the length of the Mississippi River, leaving five others with white majorities." E. Foner, Reconstruction: America's Unfinished Revolution, 1863-1877, p. 590 (1988). Some 90 years later, Alabama redefined the boundaries of the city of Tuskegee "from a square to an uncouth twenty-eight-sided figure" in a manner that was alleged to exclude black voters, and only black voters, from the city limits. *Gomillion v. Lightfoot*, 364 U. S. 339, 340 (1960).

Alabama's exercise in geometry was but one example of the racial discrimination in voting that persisted in parts of this country nearly a century after ratification of the Fifteenth Amendment. See *South Carolina v. Katzenbach*, 383 U. S. 301, 309-313 (1966). In some States, registration of eligible black voters ran 50% behind that of whites. *Id.*, at 313. Congress enacted the Voting Rights Act of 1965 as a dramatic and severe response to the situation. The Act proved immediately successful in ensuring racial minorities access to the voting booth; by the early 1970's, the spread between black and white registration in several of the targeted Southern States had fallen to well below 10%. A. Thernstrom, Whose Votes Count? Affirmative Action and Minority Voting Rights 44 (1987).

But it soon became apparent that guaranteeing equal access to the polls would not suffice to root out other racially discriminatory voting practices. Drawing on the "one person, one vote" principle, this Court recognized that "[t]he right to vote can be affected by a *dilution* of voting power as well as by an absolute prohibition on casting a ballot." *Allen v. State Bd. of Elections*, 393 U. S. 544, 569 (1969) (emphasis added). Where members of a racial minority group vote as a cohesive unit, practices such as multimember or atlarge electoral systems can reduce or nullify minority voters' ability, as a group, "to elect the candidate of their choice." *Ibid.* Accordingly, the Court held that such schemes violate the Fourteenth Amendment when they are adopted with a discriminatory purpose and have the effect of diluting minority voting strength. See, e. g., *Rogers v. Lodge*, 458 U. S. 613, 616-617 (1982); *White v. Regester*, 412 U. S. 755, 765-766 (1973). Congress, too, responded to the problem of vote dilution. In 1982, it amended § 2 of the Voting Rights Act to prohibit legislation that results in the dilution of a minority group's voting strength, regardless of the legislature's intent. 42 U. S. C. § 1973; see *Thornburg v. Gingles*, 478 U. S. 30 (1986) (applying amended § 2 to vote-dilution claim involving multimember districts); see also *Voinovich v. Quilter*, 507 U. S. 146, 155 (1993) (single-member districts).

It is against this background that we confront the questions presented here. In our view, the District Court properly dismissed appellants' claims against the federal appellees. Our focus is on appellants' claim that the State engaged in unconstitutional racial gerrymandering. That argument strikes a powerful historical chord: It is unsettling how closely the North Carolina plan resembles the most egregious racial gerrymanders of the past.

An understanding of the nature of appellants' claim is critical to our resolution of the case. In their complaint, appellants did not claim that the General Assembly's reapportionment plan unconstitutionally "diluted" white voting strength. They did not even claim to be white. Rather, appellants' complaint alleged that the deliberate segregation of voters into separate districts on the basis of race violated their constitutional right to participate in a "color-blind" electoral process. Complaint' 29, App. to Juris. Statement 89a-90a; see also Brief for Appellants 31-32.

Despite their invocation of the ideal of a "color-blind" Constitution, see *Plessy v. Ferguson*, 163 U. S. 537, 559 (1896) (Harlan, J., dissenting), appellants appear to concede that race-conscious redistricting is not always unconstitutional. See Tr. of Oral Arg. 16-19. That concession is wise: This Court never has held that race-conscious state decisionmaking is impermissible in all circumstances. What appellants object to is redistricting legislation that is so extremely irregular on its face that it rationally can be viewed only as an effort to segregate the races for purposes of voting, without regard for traditional districting principles and without sufficiently compelling justification. For the reasons that follow, we conclude that appellants have stated a claim upon which relief can be granted under the Equal Protection Clause. See Fed. Rule Civ. Proc. 12(b)(6).

The Equal Protection Clause provides that "[n]o State shall ... deny to any person within its jurisdiction the equal protection of the laws." U. S. Const., Arndt. 14, § 1. Its central purpose is to prevent the States from purposefully discriminating between individuals on the basis of race. *Washington v. Davis*, 426 U. S. 229, 239 (1976). Laws that explicitly distinguish between individuals on racial grounds fall within the core of that prohibition.

No inquiry into legislative purpose is necessary when the racial classification appears on the face of the statute. See *Personnel Administrator of Mass. v. Feeney*, 442 U. S. 256, 272 (1979). Accord, *Washington v. Seattle School Dist. No.1*, 458 U. S. 457, 485 (1982). Express racial classifications are immediately suspect because, "[a]bsent searching judicial inquiry ... , there is simply no way of determining what classifications are 'benign' or 'remedial' and what classifications are in fact motivated by illegitimate notions of racial inferiority or simple racial politics." *Richmond v. J. A. Croson Co.*, 488 U. S. 469, 493 (1989) (plurality opinion); id., at 520 (Scalia, J., concurring in judgment); see also *UJO*, 430 U. S., at 172 (Brennan, J., concurring in part) ("[A] purportedly preferential race assignment may in fact disguise a policy that perpetuates disadvantageous treatment of the plan's supposed beneficiaries").

Classifications of citizens solely on the basis of race "are by their very nature odious to a free people whose institutions are founded upon the doctrine of equality." *Hirabayas hi v. United States*, 320 U. S. 81, 100 (1943). Accord, *Loving v. Virginia*, 388 U. S. 1, 11 (1967). They threaten to stigmatize individuals by reason of their membership in a racial group and to incite racial hostility. *Croson, supra*, at 493 (plurality opinion); *UJO, supra*, at 173 (Brennan, J., concurring in part) ("[E]ven in the pursuit of remedial objectives, an explicit policy of assignment by race may serve to stimulate our society's latent race consciousness, suggesting the utility and propriety of basing decisions on a factor that ideally bears no relationship to an individual's worth or needs"). Accordingly, we have held that the Fourteenth Amendment requires state legislation that expressly distinguishes among citizens because of their race to be narrowly tailored to further a compelling governmental interest. See, e. g., *Wygant v. Jackson Bd. of Ed.*, 476 U. S. 267, 277278 (1986) (plurality opinion); *id.*, at 285 (O'Connor, J., concurring in part and concurring in judgment).

These principles apply not only to legislation that contains explicit racial distinctions, but also to those "rare" statutes that, although race neutral, are, on their face, "unexplainable on grounds other than race." *Arlington Heights v. Metropolitan Housing Development Corp.*, 429 U. S. 252, 266 (1977). As we explained in *Feeney*:

> "A racial classification, regardless of purported motivation, is presumptively invalid and can be upheld only upon an extraordinary justification. *Brown v. Board of Education*, 347 U. S. 483; *McLaughlin v. Florida*, 379 U. S. 184. This rule applies as well to a classification that is ostensibly neutral but is an obvious pretext for racial discrimination. *Yick Wo v. Hopkins*, 118 U. S. 356; *Guinn v. United States*, 238 U. S. 347; cf. *Lane v. Wilson*, 307 U. S. 268; *Gomillion v. Lightfoot*, 364 U. S. 339." 442 U. S., at 272.

Appellants contend that redistricting legislation that is so bizarre on its face that it is "unexplainable on grounds other than race," *Arlington Heights, supra,* at 266, demands the same close scrutiny that we give other state laws that classify citizens by race. Our voting rights precedents support that conclusion.

In *Guinn v. United States,* 238 U. S. 347 (1915), the Court invalidated under the Fifteenth Amendment a statute that imposed a literacy requirement on voters but contained a "grandfather clause" applicable to individuals and their lineal descendants entitled to vote "on [or prior to] January 1, 1866." *Id.,* at 357 (internal quotation marks omitted). The determinative consideration for the Court was that the law, though ostensibly race neutral, on its face "embod[ied] no exercise of judgment and rest[ed] upon no discernible reason" other than to circumvent the prohibitions of the Fifteenth Amendment. *Id.,* at 363. In other words, the statute was invalid because, on its face, it could not be explained on grounds other than race.

The Court applied the same reasoning to the "uncouth twenty-eight-sided" municipal boundary line at issue in Gomillion. Although the statute that redrew the city limits of Tuskegee was race neutral on its face, plaintiffs alleged that its effect was impermissibly to remove from the city virtually all black voters and no white voters. The Court reasoned:

> "If these allegations upon a trial remained uncontradicted or unqualified, the conclusion would be irresistible, tantamount for all practical purposes to a mathematical demonstration, that the legislation is solely concerned with segregating white

and colored voters by fencing Negro citizens out of town so as to deprive them of their pre-existing municipal vote." 364 U. S., at 341.

The majority resolved the case under the Fifteenth Amendment. *Id.*, at 342-348. Justice Whittaker, however, concluded that the "unlawful segregation of races of citizens" into different voting districts was cognizable under the Equal Protection Clause. *Id.*, at 349 (concurring opinion). This Court's subsequent reliance on *Gomillion* in other Fourteenth Amendment cases suggests the correctness of Justice Whittaker's view. See, e. g., *Feeney, supra*, at 272; *Whitcomb v. Chavis*, 403 U. S. 124, 149 (1971); see also *Mobile v. Bolden*, 446 U. S. 55, 86 (1980) (Stevens, J., concurring in judgment) (*Gomillion's* holding "is compelled by the Equal Protection Clause"). *Gomillion* thus supports appellants' contention that district lines obviously drawn for the purpose of separating voters by race require careful scrutiny under the Equal Protection Clause regardless of the motivations underlying their adoption.

The Court extended the reasoning of *Gomillion* to congressional districting in *Wright v. Rockefeller*, 376 U. S. 52 (1964). At issue in Wright were four districts contained in a New York apportionment statute. The plaintiffs alleged that the statute excluded nonwhites from one district and concentrated them in the other three. *Id.*, at 53-54. Every Member of the Court assumed that the plaintiffs' allegation that the statute "segregate[d] eligible voters by race and place of origin" stated a constitutional claim. Id., at 56 (internal quotation marks omitted); id., at 58 (Harlan, J., concurring); id., at 59-62 (Douglas, J., dissenting). The Justices disagreed only as to whether the plaintiffs had carried their burden of proof at trial. The dissenters thought the unusual shape of the district lines could "be explained only in racial terms." *Id.*, at 59. The majority, however, accepted the District Court's finding that the plaintiffs had failed to establish that the districts were in fact drawn on racial lines. Although the boundary lines were somewhat irregular, the majority reasoned, they were not so bizarre as to permit of no other conclusion. Indeed, because most of the nonwhite voters lived together in one area, it would have been difficult to construct voting districts without concentrations of nonwhite voters. *Id.*, at 56-58.

Wright illustrates the difficulty of determining from the face of a single-member districting plan that it purposefully distinguishes between voters on the basis of race. A reapportionment statute typically does not classify persons at all; it classifies tracts of land, or addresses. Moreover, redistricting differs from other kinds of state decisionmaking in that the legislature always is aware of race when it draws district lines, just as it is aware of age, economic status, religious and political persuasion, and a variety of other demographic factors. That sort of race consciousness does not lead inevitably to impermissible race discrimination. As *Wright* demonstrates, when members of a racial group live together in one community, a reapportionment plan that concentrates members of the group in one district and excludes them from others may reflect wholly legitimate purposes. The district lines may be drawn, for example, to provide for compact districts of contiguous territory, or to maintain the integrity of political subdivisions. See *Reynolds*, 377 U. S., at 578 (recognizing these as legitimate state interests).

The difficulty of proof, of course, does not mean that a racial gerrymander, once established, should receive less scrutiny under the Equal Protection Clause than other state legislation classifying citizens by race. Moreover, it seems clear to us that proof sometimes will not be difficult at all. In some exceptional cases, a reapportionment plan may be so highly irregular that, on its face, it rationally cannot be understood as anything other than an effort to "segregat[e] ... voters" on the basis of race. *Gomillion, supra*, at 341. *Gomillion*, in which a tortured municipal boundary line was drawn to exclude black voters, was such a case. So, too, would be a case in which a State concentrated a dispersed minority population in a single district by disregarding traditional districting principles such as compactness, contiguity, and respect for political subdivisions. We emphasize that these criteria are important not because they are constitutionally required— they are not, cf. *Gaffney v. Cummings*, 412 U. S. 735, 752, n. 18 (1973)—but because they are objective factors that may serve to defeat a claim that a district has been gerrymandered on racial lines. Cf. *Karcher v. Daggett*, 462 U. S. 725, 755 (1983) (Stevens, J., concurring) ("One need not use Justice Stewart's classic definition of obscenity—'I know it when I see it'—as an ultimate standard for judging the constitutionality of a gerrymander to recognize that dramatically irregular shapes may have sufficient probative force to call for an explanation" (footnotes omitted).

Put differently, we believe that reapportionment is one area in which appearances do matter. A reapportionment plan that includes in one district individuals who belong to the same race, but who are otherwise widely separated by geographical and political boundaries, and who may have little in common with one another but the color of their skin, bears an uncomfortable resemblance to political apartheid. It reinforces the perception that members of the same racial group—regardless of their age, education, economic status, or the community in which they live—think alike, share the same political interests, and will prefer the same candidates at the polls. We have rejected such perceptions elsewhere as impermissible racial stereotypes. See, e. g., *Holland v. Illinois*, 493 U. S. 474, 484, n. 2 (1990) ("[A] prosecutor's assumption that a black juror may be presumed to be partial simply because he is black ... violates the Equal Protection Clause" (internal quotation marks omitted)); see also *Edmonson v. Leesville Concrete Co.*, 500 U. S. 614, 630-631 (1991) ("If our society is to continue to progress as a multiracial democracy, it must recognize that the automatic invocation of race stereotypes retards that progress and causes continued hurt and injury"). By perpetuating such notions, a racial gerrymander may exacerbate the very patterns of racial bloc voting that majority-minority districting is sometimes said to counteract.

The message that such districting sends to elected representatives is equally pernicious. When a district obviously is created solely to effectuate the perceived common interests of one racial group, elected officials are more likely to believe that their primary obligation is to represent only the members of that group, rather than their constituency as a whole. This is altogether antithetical to our system of representative democracy. As Justice Douglas explained in his dissent in *Wright v. Rockefeller* nearly 30 years ago:

"Here the individual is important, not his race, his creed, or his color. The principle of equality is at war with the notion that District A must be represented by a Negro, as it is with the notion that District B must be represented by a Caucasian, District C by a Jew, District D by a Catholic, and so on .... That system, by whatever name it is called, is a divisive force in a community, emphasizing differences between candidates and voters that are irrelevant in the constitutional sense ....

"When racial or religious lines are drawn by the State, the multiracial, multireligious communities that our Constitution seeks to weld together as one become separatist; antagonisms that relate to race or to religion rather than to political issues are generated; communities seek not the best representative but the best racial or religious partisan. Since that system is at war with the democratic ideal, it should find no footing here." 376 U. S., at 66-67.

For these reasons, we conclude that a plaintiff challenging a reapportionment statute under the Equal Protection Clause may state a claim by alleging that the legislation, though race neutral on its face, rationally cannot be understood as anything other than an effort to separate voters into different districts on the basis of race, and that the separation lacks sufficient justification. It is unnecessary for us to decide whether or how a reapportionment plan that, on its face, can be explained in nonracial terms successfully could be challenged. Thus, we express no view as to whether "the intentional creation of majority-minority districts, without more," always gives rise to an equal protection claim. *Post*, at 668 (White, J., dissenting). We hold only that, on the facts of this case, appellants have stated a claim sufficient to defeat the state appellees' motion to dismiss.

The dissenters consider the circumstances of this case "functionally indistinguishable" from multimember districting and at-large voting systems, which are loosely described as "other varieties of gerrymandering." *Post*, at 671 (W, J., dissenting); see also *post*, at 684 (Souter, J., dissenting). We have considered the constitutionality of these practices in other Fourteenth Amendmehitent cases and have required plaintiffs to demonstrate that the challenged practice has the purpose and effect of diluting a racial group's voting strength. See, e. g., *Rogers v. Lodge*, 458 U. S. 613 (1982) (at-large system); *Mobile v. Bolden*, 446 U. S. 55 (1980) (same); *White v. Regester*, 412 U. S. 755 (1973) (multimember districts); *Whitcomb v. Chavis*, 403 U. S. 124 (1971) (same); see also *supra*, at 640-641. At-large and multimember schemes, however, do not classify voters on the basis of race. Classifying citizens by race, as we have said, threatens special harms that are not present in our vote-dilution cases. It therefore warrants different analysis.

Justice Souter apparently believes that racial gerrymandering is harmless unless it dilutes a racial group's voting strength. See *post*, at 684 (dissenting opinion). As we have explained, however, reapportionment legislation that cannot be understood as anything other than an effort to classify and separate voters by race injures voters in other ways. It reinforces racial stereotypes and threatens to undermine our system of representative democracy by signaling to elected officials that they represent a particular racial group rather than their constituency as a whole. See *supra*, at 647-649. Justice Souter does not adequately explain why these harms are not cognizable under the Fourteenth Amendment.

The dissenters make two other arguments that cannot be reconciled with our precedents. First, they suggest that a racial gerrymander of the sort alleged here is functionally equivalent to gerrymanders for nonracial purposes, such as political gerrymanders. See *post*, at 679 (opinion of Stevens, J.); see also *post*, at 662-663 (opinion of White, J.). This Court has held political gerrymanders to be justiciable under the Equal Protection Clause. See *Davis v. Bandemer*, 478 U. S., at 118-127. But nothing in our case law compels the conclusion that racial and political gerrymanders are subject to precisely the same constitutional scrutiny. In fact, our country's long and persistent history of racial discrimination in voting—as well as our Fourteenth Amendment jurisprudence, which always has reserved the strictest scrutiny for discrimination on the basis of race, see *supra*, at 642-644—would seem to compel the opposite conclusion.

Second, Justice Stevens argues that racial gerrymandering poses no constitutional difficulties when district lines are drawn to favor the minority, rather than the majority. See *post*, at 678 (dissenting opinion). We have made clear, however, that equal protection analysis "is not dependent on the race of those burdened or benefited by a particular classification." *Croson*, 488 U. S., at 494 (plurality opinion); see also *id.*, at 520 (Scalia, J., concurring in judgment). Accord, *Wygant,* 476 U. S., at 273 (plurality opinion). Indeed, racial classifications receive close scrutiny even when they may be said to burden or benefit the races equally. See *Powers v. Ohio,* 499 U. S. 400, 410 (1991) ("It is axiomatic that racial classifications do not become legitimate on the assumption that all persons suffer them in equal degree").

Finally, nothing in the Court's highly fractured decision in *UJO*—on which the District Court almost exclusively relied, and which the dissenters evidently believe controls, see *post,* at 664-667 (opinion of White, J.); *post,* at 684, and n. 6 (opinion of Souter, J.)—forecloses the claim we recognize today. *UJO* concerned New York's revision of a reapportionment plan to include additional majority-minority districts in response to the Attorney General's denial of administrative preclearance under § 5. In that regard, it closely resembles the present case. But the cases are critically different in another way. The plaintiffs in *UJO*—members of a Hasidic community split between two districts under New York's revised redistricting plan—did not allege that the plan, on its face, was so highly irregular that it rationally could be understood only as an effort to segregate voters by race. Indeed, the facts of the case would not have supported such a claim. Three Justices approved the New York statute, in part, precisely because it adhered to traditional districting principles:

> "[We think it ... permissible for a State, *employing sound districting principles such as compactness and population equality,* to attempt to prevent racial minorities from being repeatedly outvoted

by creating districts that will afford fair representation to the members of those racial groups who
are sufficiently numerous *and whose residential
patterns afford the opportunity* of creating districts
in which they will be in the majority." 430 U. S., at
168 (opinion of White, J., joined by Stevens and
Rehenquist, JJ.)

As a majority of the Justices construed the
complaint, the *UJO* plaintiffs made a different claim: that
the New York plan impermissibly "diluted" their voting
strength. Five of the eight Justices who participated in the
decision resolved the case under the framework the Court
previously had adopted for vote-dilution cases. Three
Justices rejected the plaintiffs' claim on the grounds that
the New York statute "represented no racial slur or stigma
with respect to whites or any other race" and left white
voters with better than proportional representation. *Id.*,
at 165-166. Two others concluded that the statute did not
minimize or cancel out a minority group's voting strength
and that the State's intent to comply with the Voting
Rights Act, as interpreted by the Department of Justice,
"foreclose[d] any finding that [the State] acted with the
invidious purpose of discriminating against white voters."
Id., at 180 (Stewart, J., joined by Powell, J., concurring
in judgment).

The District Court below relied on these portions
of UJO to reject appellants' claim. See 808 F. Supp., at
472-473. In our view, the court used the wrong analysis.
UJO's framework simply does not apply where, as here,
a reapportionment plan is alleged to be so irrational on
its face that it immediately offends principles of racial
equality. *UJO* set forth a standard under which white

voters can establish unconstitutional vote dilution. But it did not purport to overrule *Gomillion or Wright.* Nothing in the decision precludes white voters (or voters of any other race) from bringing the analytically distinct claim that a reapportionment plan rationally cannot be understood as anything other than an effort to segregate citizens into separate voting districts on the basis of race without sufficient justification. Because appellants here stated such a claim, the District Court erred in dismissing their complaint.

Justice Souter contends that exacting scrutiny of racial gerrymanders under the Fourteenth Amendment is inappropriate because reapportionment "nearly always require[s] some consideration of race for legitimate reasons." *Post*, at 680 (dissenting opinion). "As long as members of racial groups have [a] commonality of interest" and "racial bloc voting takes place," he argues, "legislators will have to take race into account" in order to comply with the Voting Rights Act. *Ibid.* Justice Souter's reasoning is flawed.

Earlier this Term, we unanimously reaffirmed that racial bloc voting and minority-group political cohesion never can be assumed, but specifically must be proved in each case in order to establish that a redistricting plan dilutes minority voting strength in violation of § 2. See *Growe v. Emison*, 507 U. S. 25, 40-41 (1993) ("Unless these points are established, there neither has been a wrong nor can be a remedy"). That racial bloc voting or minority political cohesion may be found to exist in some cases, of course, is no reason to treat all racial gerrymanders differently from other kinds of racial classification. Justice Souter apparently views racial gerrymandering of the type presented here as a special category of "benign" racial discrimination that should be subject to relaxed judicial review. Cf. *post*, at 684-685 (dissenting opinion). As we have said, however, the very reason that the Equal Protection Clause demands strict scrutiny of all racial classifications is because without it, a court cannot determine whether or not the discrimination truly is "benign." See *supra*, at 642-643. Thus, if appellants' allegations of a racial gerrymander are not contradicted on remand, the District Court must determine whether the General Assembly's reapportionment plan satisfies strict scrutiny. We therefore consider what that level of scrutiny requires in the reapportionment context.

The state appellees suggest that a covered jurisdiction may have a compelling interest in creating majority-minority districts in order to comply with the Voting Rights Act. The States certainly have a very strong interest in complying with federal antidiscrimination laws that are constitutionally valid as interpreted and as applied. But in the context of a Fourteenth Amendment challenge, courts must bear in mind the difference between what the law permits and what it requires.

For example, on remand North Carolina might claim that it adopted the revised plan in order to comply with the § 5 "nonretrogression" principle. Under that principle, a proposed voting change cannot be precleared if it will lead to "a retrogression in the position of racial minorities with respect to their effective exercise of the electoral franchise." *Beer v. United States*, 425 U. S. 130, 141 (1976). In *Beer*, we held that a reapportionment plan that created one majority minority district where none existed before passed muster under § 5 because it

CRITICAL PERSPECTIVES ON GERRYMANDERING

improved the position of racial minorities. *Id.*, at 141-142; see also *Richmond v. United States*, 422 U. S. 358, 370-371 (1975) (annexation that reduces percentage of blacks in population satisfies § 5 where postannexation districts "fairly reflect" current black voting strength).

Although the Court concluded that the redistricting scheme at issue in *Beer* was nonretrogressive, it did not hold that the plan, for that reason, was immune from constitutional challenge. The Court expressly declined to reach that question. See 425 U. S., at 142, n. 14. Indeed, the Voting Rights Act and our case law make clear that a reapportionment plan that satisfies § 5 still may be enjoined as unconstitutional. See 42 U. S. C. § 1973c (neither a declaratory judgment by the District Court for the District of Columbia nor preclearance by the Attorney General "shall bar a subsequent action to enjoin enforcement" of new voting practice); Allen, 393 U. S., at 549-550 (after preclearance, "private parties may enjoin the enforcement of the new enactment ... in traditional suits attacking its constitutionality"). Thus, we do not read *Beer* or any of our other § 5 cases to give covered jurisdictions *carte blanche* to engage in racial gerrymandering in the name of nonretrogression. A reapportionment plan would not be narrowly tailored to the goal of avoiding retrogression if the State went beyond what was reasonably necessary to avoid retrogression. Our conclusion is supported by the plurality opinion in *UJO*, in which four Justices determined that New York's creation of additional majority-minority districts was constitutional because the plaintiffs had failed to demonstrate that the State "did more than the Attorney General was authorized to *require* it to do under the nonretrogression principle of *Beer*." 430

U. S., at 162-163 (opinion of White, J., joined by Brennan, Blackmun, and Stevens, JJ.) (emphasis added).

Before us, the state appellees contend that the General Assembly's revised plan was necessary not to prevent retrogression, but to avoid dilution of black voting strength in violation of § 2, as construed in *Thornburg v. Gingles*, 478 U. S. 30 (1986). In *Gingles* the Court considered a multimember redistricting plan for the North Carolina State Legislature. The Court held that members of a racial minority group claiming § 2 vote dilution through the use of multimember districts must prove three threshold conditions: that the minority group "is sufficiently large and geographically compact to constitute a majority in a single-member district," that the minority group is "politically cohesive," and that "the white majority votes sufficiently as a bloc to enable it ... usually to defeat the minority's preferred candidate." *Id.*, at 50-51. We have indicated that similar preconditions apply in § 2 challenges to single-member districts. See *Voinovich v. Quilter*, 507 U. S., at 157-158; *Growe v. Emison*, 507 U. S., at 40.

Appellants maintain that the General Assembly's revised plan could not have been required by § 2. They contend that the State's black population is too dispersed to support two geographically compact majority-black districts, as the bizarre shape of District 12 demonstrates, and that there is no evidence of black political cohesion. They also contend that recent black electoral successes demonstrate the willingness of white voters in North Carolina to vote for black candidates. Appellants point out that blacks currently hold the positions of State Auditor, Speaker of the North Carolina House of Representatives, and chair of the North

Carolina State Board of Elections. They also point out that in 1990 a black candidate defeated a white opponent in the Democratic Party runoff for a United States Senate seat before being defeated narrowly by the Republican incumbent in the general election. Appellants further argue that if § 2 did require adoption of North Carolina's revised plan, § 2 is to that extent unconstitutional. These arguments were not developed below, and the issues remain open for consideration on remand.

The state appellees alternatively argue that the General Assembly's plan advanced a compelling interest entirely distinct from the Voting Rights Act. We previously have recognized a significant state interest in eradicating the effects of past racial discrimination. See, e. g., *Croson*, 488 U. S., at 491-493 (opinion of O'Connor, J., joined by Rehnquist, C. J., and White, J.); *id.*, at 518 (Kennedy, J., concurring in part and concurring in judgment); *Wygant*, 476 U. S., at 280282 (plurality opinion); id., at 286 (O'Connor, J., concurring in part and concurring in judgment). But the State must have a "'strong basis in evidence for [concluding] that remedial action [is] necessary.'" *Croson*, supra, at 500 (quoting *Wygant, supra*, at 277 (plurality opinion)).

The state appellees submit that two pieces of evidence gave the General Assembly a strong basis for believing that remedial action was warranted here: the Attorney General's imposition of the § 5 preclearance requirement on 40 North Carolina counties, and the *Gingles* District Court's findings of a long history of official racial discrimination in North Carolina's political system and of pervasive racial bloc voting. The state appellees assert that the deliberate creation of majority-minority districts is the most precise way—indeed the only effective way—to overcome the effects of racially polarized voting. This question also need not be decided at this stage of the litigation. We note, however, that only three Justices in *UJO* were prepared to say that States have a significant interest in minimizing the consequences of racial bloc voting apart from the requirements of the Voting Rights Act. And those three Justices specifically concluded that race-based districting, as a response to racially polarized voting, is constitutionally permissible only when the State "employ[s] sound districting principles," and only when the affected racial group's "residential patterns afford the opportunity of creating districts in which they will be in the majority." 430 U. S., at 167-168 (opinion of White, J., joined by Stevens and Rehnquist, JJ.).

Racial classifications of any sort pose the risk of lasting harm to our society. They reinforce the belief, held by too many for too much of our history, that individuals should be judged by the color of their skin. Racial classifications with respect to voting carry particular dangers. Racial gerrymandering, even for remedial purposes, may balkanize us into competing racial factions; it threatens to carry us further from the goal of a political system in which race no longer matters—a goal that the Fourteenth and Fifteenth Amendments embody, and to which the Nation continues to aspire. It is for these reasons that race-based districting by our state legislatures demands close judicial scrutiny.

In this case, the Attorney General suggested that North Carolina could have created a reasonably compact second majority-minority district in the south-central to southeastern part of the State. We express no view as to whether appellants successfully could have challenged such a district under the Fourteenth Amendment. We also do not decide whether appellants' complaint stated a claim under constitutional provisions other than the Fourteenth Amendment. Today we hold only that appellants have stated a claim under the Equal Protection Clause by alleging that the North Carolina General Assembly adopted a reapportionment scheme so irrational on its face that it can be understood only as an effort to segregate voters into separate voting districts because of their race, and that the separation lacks sufficient justification. If the allegation of racial gerrymandering remains uncontradicted, the District Court further must determine whether the North Carolina plan is narrowly tailored to further a compelling governmental interest. Accordingly, we reverse the judgment of the District Court and remand the case for further proceedings consistent with this opinion.

It is so ordered.

1. The justices in this case found that racial gerrymandering must be held to strict scrutiny because it violates the equal protection clause. How does gerrymandering violate equal protection? Do you think only racially based gerrymandering violates this clause, or would partisan gerrymandering also be in violation? Explain.

EXCERPT FROM *GILL V. WHITFORD*: WISCONSIN'S PARTISAN GERRYMANDERING CASE, BY STACI DUROS, 2017

PARTISAN GERRYMANDERING AND ITS FOUNDATIONAL CASE LAW

BRIEF OVERVIEW OF PARTISAN GERRYMANDERING

To *gerrymander* is to draw political districts in such a way as to ensure political gain.[66] *Partisan gerrymandering* [67] is the drawing of electoral district lines by the party in power in a manner that intentionally discriminates and disadvantages the opposing political party. The effect of partisan gerrymandering is the tendency of the state to lean in a certain political direction for the duration of the redistricting map. Partisan gerrymandering takes the form of two basic techniques that work in tandem: *packing* the opposition's supporters into a handful of districts, where they win in landslides, and *cracking* them among multiple districts, where they lose by slim margins. The goal of either technique is to dilute the voting strength of a *voting bloc*, effectively denying the opportunity of that group to elect a representative of its choice. Cracking divides voters of the same characteristic into multiple districts. This technique denies these voters a large enough voting bloc in any particular district. For example, voters in an urban area could be divided among several, surrounding suburban or rural districts.[68] Packing concentrates as many voters of the same characteristic into a single electoral district, or into as few districts as possible. Packing may sometimes be done to ensure representation for a community of common interest. For example, a *majority-minority district* [69] may be created to remedy or avoid violations of Section 2 of the Voting Rights Acts of 1965.

Partisan gerrymanders use cracking and packing techniques in tandem to maximize the gerrymandering party's electoral advantage. When voters are cracked, their community is split into multiple districts to ensure that their voting strength is diluted enough to pose no significant challenge in any one of the districts. Their voting strength is, in effect, diluted because their votes are cast without the possibility of overcoming the opposing majority. Packed voters face the opposite problem. If there are too many districts that contain the opposing party's voters, the gerrymandering party tries to limit their potential damage by drawing them all into one district (or into as few districts as possible). Their voting strength is concentrated in the packed district and reduced in the other districts. The gerrymandering party then spreads out their own party's voters in such a way as to win multiple seats in order to have a comfortable majority in the legislature.

The ability to choose where to place boundaries for legislative districts affects which voters candidates will be responsible to on Election Day. To assess advantage for the gerrymandering party, underlying partisan strength of districts is measured and evaluated using historical electoral data. Then that data is used to forecast election results in prospective districts. Therefore, the district boundaries become the most important factor in determining representation, meaning who will win and by how many votes, because a political party can manipulate those lines for its own partisan advantage.

Most partisan gerrymanders are constitutionally challenged as a violation of the equal protection clause of the Fourteenth Amendment and the "one person, one vote" principle because partisan gerrymandering unfairly dilutes the opposing party's voters' ability to elect representatives who support their interests.[70] The typical partisan gerrymander argument states that no matter how much effort the opposing party puts into getting itself elected, the maps are so skewed in favor of the gerrymandering party that even if the opposing party gets more votes, the gerrymandering party retains its majority power. In other words, partisan gerrymandering creates representational asymmetry between major political parties.

Courts have heard partisan gerrymandering challenges in the past; however, no judicial standard exists to determine an unconstitutional disadvantage created by a partisan gerrymander. The existence (or lack thereof) of an objective judicial standard forms the basis of the foundational case history on partisan gerrymandering. It is necessary to discuss each case because *Whitford v. Gill* builds on the precedents of the Supreme Court of the United States.

JUSTICIABILITY AND MEASURING UNCONSTITUTIONALITY

Even if partisan gerrymandering was alleged in a given case, population equality and racial discrimination dominated constitutional challenges in redistricting cases. However, without directly speaking to the justiciability of partisan gerrymandering, "invidious discrimination" in reapportionment had been raised in the cases of Fortson v. Dorsey [71] and Burns v. Richardson.[72] In White v. Regester, the Supreme Court has held that multimember districts violate the Constitution when plaintiffs have produced evidence that an election was "not equally open to participation by the group in question—that members had less opportunity than did other residents in the district to participate in the political processes and to elect legislators of their choice."[73] In Gaffney v. Cummings,[74] the Supreme Court stated:

> [J]udicial interest should be at its lowest ebb when a state purports fairly to allocate political power to the parties in accordance with their voting strength and, within quite tolerable limits, succeeds in doing so ... neither we nor the district courts have a constitutional warrant to invalidate a state plan, otherwise within tolerable population limits, because it undertakes, not to minimize or eliminate the political strength of any group or party, but to recognize it and, through districting, provide a rough sort of proportional representation in the legislative halls of the State.[75]

Although these cases mainly focused on discriminatory apportionment that rely on voting strength dilution, they indicate that vote-dilution cases are governed by the same standards as other equal protection claims in that the plaintiffs must establish both a discriminatory intent and discriminatory effect. Absent those demonstrable two factors, the equal protection clause was not violated.

The Supreme Court has heard two major partisan gerrymandering claims that exclusively deal with partisan gerrymandering, and these two cases provide the foundation for *Whitford v. Gill.*

DAVIS V. BANDEMER

In 1986, the Supreme Court heard the first case, *Davis v. Bandemer*, 478 U.S. 109 (1986),[76] in which a political party directly raised, and the Court squarely addressed, a claim that a legislative redistricting plan invidiously discriminated against members of an opposing political party. In *Davis v. Bandemer*, Indiana Democrats challenged the 1981 state redistricting plan passed by a Republican-controlled legislature. The plaintiffs alleged that the redistricting plan had been drawn in such a way as to disadvantage Indiana Democratic voters in electing representatives of their choosing, in violation of the equal protection clause, under the Fourteenth Amendment of the U.S. Constitution. A three-judge panel of the United States District Court for the Southern District of Indiana found that Indiana Democrats were a "politically salient class," whose "proportionate voting influence . . . [had been] adversely affected."[77] The district court also found that the State of Indiana was unable to justify that the map was "supported by adequate neutral criteria" and so they ruled that the map was an unconstitutional gerrymandering.[78] The defendants then appealed to the Supreme Court.

The Supreme Court came to a number of important conclusions even though it ultimately overruled the lower court's decision. For the first time, it explicitly stated that it "f[ound] . . . political gerrymandering to be justiciable."[79]

Agreeing with the district court, a plurality[80] of the Supreme Court held for the first time that a plan that discriminated against an "identifiable political group," proving "both intentional discrimination . . . and an actual discriminatory effect on that group," could be challenged as unconstitutional under the equal protection clause of the Fourteenth Amendment.[81] According to the Court, "[u]nconstitutional discrimination occurs only when the electoral system is arranged in a manner that will *consistently degrade a voter's or group of voters' influence on the political process as a whole*."[82] The plurality also agreed with the lower court's finding of discriminatory intent, stating that "[a]s long as redistricting is done by a legislature it should not be very difficult to prove that the likely political consequences of the reapportionment were intended."[83] Discriminatory intent still had to be proven by the plaintiffs. The Court made sure to include that political influence is not limited to winning elections, stating that "a group's electoral power is not unconstitutionally diminished by the simple fact of an apportionment scheme that makes winning elections more difficult."[84]

However, the Court did not rule in the plaintiffs' favor by striking down the maps. The Supreme Court overruled the decision made by the district court that had declared the maps unconstitutional because the plaintiffs had failed to show that the district plan was "sufficiently adverse" to constitute a constitutional violation of the equal protection clause. The plurality opinion[85] suggested that a partisan gerrymander would be unconstitutional only if it left the disadvantaged party without any means of influence, or a fair opportunity for electoral success over many election cycles,[86] adding that "such a finding of unconstitutionality must be supported by evidence of continued frustration of the will of a majority of voters or effective denial to a minority of voters of a fair chance to influence the political process."[87] The evidence for long-lasting results was missing from the *Bandemer* trial record and informed the plurality's opinion:

> Relying on a single election to prove unconstitutional discrimination is unsatisfactory. The District Court observed, and the parties do not disagree, that Indiana is a swing State. Voters sometimes prefer Democratic candidates, and sometimes Republican. The District Court did not find that because of the 1981 Act the Democrats could not in one of the next few elections secure a sufficient vote to take control of the assembly. Indeed, the District Court declined to hold that the 1982 election results were the predictable consequences of the 1981 Act and expressly refused to hold that those results were a reliable prediction of future ones. The District Court did not ask by what percentage the statewide Democratic vote would have had to increase to control either the House or the Senate. The appellants argue here, without a persuasive response from the appellees, that had the Democratic candidates received an additional few percentage points of the votes cast statewide, they would have obtained a majority of the seats in both houses. Nor was there any finding that the 1981 reapportionment would consign the Democrats to a minority status in the Assembly throughout the 1980s or that the Democrats would have no hope of doing any better in the reapportionment that would occur after the 1990 census.

Without findings of this nature, the District Court erred in concluding that the 1981 Act violated the Equal Protection Clause.[88]

Partisan gerrymandering did violate the equal protection clause. However, in order to prove it, plaintiffs must demonstrate the drafter's intent, effect, and predictably long-lasting results in its consequences. These three items have come to be known collectively as the "Bandemer Test."

TABLE 2. THE BANDEMER TEST

1. **Intent**—an established purpose to create a legislative districting map that purposefully disempowers voters of one political party.

2. **Effect**—proof that an election on a contested map resulted in a distorted outcome.

3. **Predictably long-lasting results in its consequences**— evidentiary election data that proves dilution of votes, meaning noncompetitive elections, reliable projections of future results, seat losses for the minority party, etc.

In the subsequent twenty years after this case, no challenged redistricting plan has been held as unconstitutional on partisan grounds. In *Vieth v. Jubelirer*, the Supreme Court revisited the issue of partisan gerrymandering for the second time in eighteen years.

VIETH V. JUBELIRER

In 2004, the Supreme Court heard the case *Vieth v. Jubelirer*, 541 U.S. 267 (2004). The plaintiffs, Democratic voters in Pennsylvania, challenged the congressional redistricting plan, enacted by the Republican-controlled legislature, alleging that it benefited Republican candidates at the expense of Democrats. Specifically, the plaintiffs argued that the plan violated the "one person, one vote" principle of Article I of the Constitution, the equal protection clause of the Fourteenth Amendment, the privileges and immunities clause of Article IV of the Constitution, and the freedom of association guaranteed by the First Amendment. A three-judge panel of the U.S. District Court for the Middle District of Pennsylvania threw out the redistricting plan because it contained districts of unequal population.[89] The Pennsylvania Legislature corrected the population disparities, and the Democrats once again challenged the new district plan using the same list of violations. This time the district court, finding no violation of the "one person, one vote" principle and again dismissing the other claims (equal protection clause of the Fourteenth Amendment, the privileges and immunities clause of Article IV of the Constitution), upheld the redistricting plan. The Democrats then appealed to the Supreme Court. The Supreme Court's plurality opinion held that partisan gerrymandering was a political question that was off-limits to the courts because there are no "judicially discernible and manageable standards" for gauging when drafters took redistricting too far.[90]

> Eighteen years of judicial effort with virtually nothing to show for it justify us in revisiting the question whether the standard promised by *Bandemer* exists. As the following discussion reveals, no judicially discernible and manageable standards for adjudicating political gerrymandering claims have emerged. Lacking them, we must conclude that political gerrymandering claims are nonjusticiable and that *Bandemer* was wrongly decided.[91]

Four other justices[92] disagreed, arguing that courts could intervene in partisan gerrymandering cases and proposing various tests for determining when a partisan gerrymander had occurred. Falling somewhere in the middle of these two opinions, Justice Anthony Kennedy affirmed that partisan gerrymandering is an issue courts can decide, but said none of the proposed standards were sufficient, leaving open the question of what standards courts should use when evaluating those claims.

A decision ordering the correction of all election district lines drawn for partisan reasons would commit federal and state courts to unprecedented intervention in the American political process. The Court is correct to refrain from directing this substantial intrusion into the Nation's political life. While agreeing with the plurality that the complaint the appellants filed in the District Court must be dismissed, and while understanding that great caution is necessary when approaching this subject, I would not foreclose all possibility of judicial relief if some limited and precise rationale were found to correct an established violation of the Constitution in some redistricting cases.[93]

Despite the finding that no standard currently existed, the Fourteenth Amendment, and possibly the First Amendment, still provided some general standard for constitutionality that the Court could use as a basis for determining when political groups' representational rights have been unconstitutionally burdened.[94] The *Vieth* decision has caused problems for lower courts and litigants.[95]

LEAGUE OF LATIN AMERICAN CITIZENS (LULAC) V. PERRY

Two years after *Vieth*, *LULAC v. Perry*, 548 U.S. 399 (2006)[96] represented the Supreme Court's third and most recent attempt to create a reliable standard for adjudicating claims of partisan gerrymandering. The plaintiffs claimed that Texas's 2003 congressional redistricting plan not only violated Section 2 of the Voting Rights Act of 1965 but also was an unconstitutional partisan gerrymander. As in *Vieth*, the Supreme Court was once again divided, producing six separate concurrences.[97]

The Court did not directly address the issue of justiciability of partisan gerrymandering claims.[98] Instead of expressing a particular partisan gerrymandering standard for the lower courts and political branches of state government, the Court examined the plaintiffs' proposed standard. The plaintiffs' standard centered on the motivation to decide to adopt a redistricting plan mid-decade, concluding that the decision had no other motive than to disadvantage the opposing political party and this was enough to prove a claim of unconstitutional partisan gerrymandering.[99]

Writing for the majority, Justice Kennedy rejected the plaintiffs' argument concerning mid-decade redistricting, arguing that "there is nothing inherently suspect about a legislature's decision to replace mid-decade a court-ordered plan with one of its own."[100] In addition, the Court added that "a successful claim attempting to identify unconstitutional acts of partisan gerrymandering must do what appellants' sole motivation theory explicitly disavows: show a burden, as measured by a reliable standard, on the complainants' representational rights."[101] The Supreme Court distinguished two separate challenges that a plaintiff must overcome for a successful partisan gerrymandering constitutional challenge: demonstrate a reliable measure of partisan dominance a plan achieves in its intent and effect as well as "a standard for deciding how much partisan dominance is too much."[102]

As of the time of publication of this article over a decade after *LULAC*, the Supreme Court still does not have a manageable standard. While the Court has recognized that partisan gerrymandering can be unconstitutional, a constitutional challenge has yet to succeed on that ground because plaintiffs have been unable to offer a workable standard to distinguish between permissible political line-drawing and unconstitutional partisan gerrymandering.

1. In a previous case mentioned by the author, the US Supreme Court determined that it could not hear a case on partisan gerrymandering because it was impossible to determine when political redistricting was taken too far. After

having read the cases presented here, do you agree with that decision? Explain.

2. There is currently, according to the author and the Supreme Court, no basis for determining if partisan redistricting has gone too far. What are some signs you would look for to determine if a redistricting is fair or is partisan and therefore problematic?

"IS PARTISAN GERRYMANDERING ILLEGAL? THE SUPREME COURT WILL DECIDE," BY JONATHAN ENTIN, FROM *THE CONVERSATION*, SEPTEMBER 27, 2017

One of the first cases that the Supreme Court will hear this term could make a huge difference in how legislative and congressional districts are drawn. In Gill v. Whitford, Wisconsin Democrats claim that Republicans drew lines that virtually guarantee GOP control of both houses of the state legislature.

A lower court struck down the Wisconsin districting system as an unconstitutional partisan gerrymander – an impermissible manipulation of district lines for the benefit of the party in power. A Supreme Court decision upholding that ruling could prevent the party in control of each state's redistricting process from drawing lines in its favor.

This case will force the Supreme Court to tackle questions that have long gone unanswered. Can the courts actually rule on partisan gerrymandering? And if so, how will they evaluate such claims?

RISE OF THE GERRYMANDER

Partisanship always has been a big factor in redistricting. The term gerrymandering was coined in 1812, after Massachusetts Gov. Elbridge Gerry approved a plan in which one district was shaped like a salamander. Both parties have tried to manipulate district lines to their own advantage ever since.

Two recent factors have led to increased concern about partisan gerrymandering all over the country. Sophisticated software makes it easy to manipulate the lines for partisan advantage. And growing ideological polarization between the parties encourages them to do that. In the past couple of years, lawsuits over partisan gerrymandering have cropped up in Maryland, North Carolina, Texas and Virginia.

The Supreme Court has never struck down a partisan gerrymander, but it has rejected other districting manipulations. The "one-person, one-vote" principle means districts should be roughly equal, so that everyone's vote is equal. And racial gerrymandering is impermissible.

This is what makes the Wisconsin case so noteworthy. Its potential impact might explain why more than 50 amicus briefs have been filed by a wide range of groups whose interests could be affected by whatever decision the Supreme Court makes.

WHO DECIDES?

In Gill v. Whitford, the justices face two important questions.

First, may courts even consider partisan gerrymandering claims? The Supreme Court has given mixed signals here. A 1986 case, for example, ruled that courts could consider partisan gerrymandering, but found no constitutional defect in Indiana's legislative districts. But in another case from Pennsylvania in 2004, four justices concluded that courts could not consider partisan gerrymandering claims, while a fifth rejected the challenge on the merits.

Finding a manageable legal standard for partisan gerrymandering might be more complicated than it is for other districting problems. In one-person, one-vote cases, for instance, a court can look at population differences between districts.

Racial gerrymandering disputes can be complicated, but courts have devised rough and ready tests. The Supreme Court had no trouble striking down the Alabama legislature's almost surgical redrawing of Tuskegee's boundaries to remove virtually every black voter from the city while leaving every white voter in place.

But in places with racially polarized voting, it can be challenging to tell whether a case involves a racial gerrymander or a partisan gerrymander. Although the Wisconsin case doesn't really pose this problem, it has arisen in many others.

TESTING THE BOUNDARIES

Still, if we accept that districting is "fundamentally a political affair," as Justice Sandra Day O'Connor once put it, how much partisan manipulation is too much? Any answer to that question involves some type of statistical analysis, and courts are not terribly comfortable with math.

Some states require that their districts be compact and contiguous, meaning that they have more or less regular shapes and that all parts of the district are geographically connected.

However, that's not explicitly embodied in federal law. The Wisconsin Democrats have offered a relatively simple index called the efficiency gap as a measure of partisan gerrymandering. This index estimates how many voters are packed into safe districts, instead of being spread out to make more districts competitive.

A number of leading scholars, including the expert used by Wisconsin Republicans in drawing the state's legislative districts, contend that there are other generally accepted methods for evaluating partisan gerrymandering claims. For example, a partisan symmetry test would explore whether one party has to get more votes than the other party in order to win the same number of seats.

But the Wisconsin parties disagree about that contention. The Republicans contend that these tests are too complex and fail to provide a "limited and precise" standard for evaluating partisan gerrymandering claims.

CONSTITUTIONALITY

This gets us to the second question that the Supreme Court might have to address. If the justices agree that courts may decide partisan gerrymandering cases, they then will have to determine whether the Wisconsin districting system violates the Constitution.

The Constitution doesn't say anything explicit about gerrymandering of any kind. The basic argument against it says that partisan gerrymandering is inconsistent with basic concepts of self-government. Parties who challenge partisan gerrymandering couch their arguments in terms of the Due Process and Equal Protection Clauses of the 14th Amendment. Some commentators also have suggested that partisan gerrymandering violates the First Amendment.

This means the Supreme Court will have to decide whether the lower court's decision to reject the Wisconsin district lines was legally sound. The justices could uphold that decision. Or they could decide that the lower court used an incorrect legal standard and remand the case for further consideration under the correct standard.

POTENTIAL IMPACT

The stakes in this case are enormous. If the Wisconsin Democrats win, we should expect the minority party in many states to sue over redistricting plans that advantage the majority party. This already happens in one-person, one-vote disputes, as well as in claims of racial gerrymandering.

But if the Wisconsin Republicans win, we can expect even more partisan manipulation in redistricting, a process which must be done after every census. This will make it easier for representatives to choose their voters rather than for voters to choose their representatives.

Neither outcome provides grounds for optimism. Either court proceedings will generate uncertainty over district lines or politicians will maneuver for partisan advantage.

Maybe this Wisconsin case will encourage greater use of independent commissions for redistricting. This is how Arizona, California, Idaho and Washington do it. And the Supreme Court in 2015 upheld the Arizona system against a constitutional challenge. Or we might devise other ways to elect legislators.

But let's not be naïve. Politics, as Mr. Dooley long ago explained, ain't beanbag. How district lines are drawn is only part of the problem of promotingresponsible government.

1. The author talks about whether the US Supreme Court can hear a case about gerrymandering, since the Supreme Court primarily decides constitutional matters. Based on what you've read in this and other articles, should the Supreme Court hear this case?

2. The author discusses how partisan gerrymandering is considered a different issue from racial gerrymandering, which has been struck down as unfair by the courts. Do you think these should be considered different matters? Explain.

"A SUPREME COURT CASE COULD MAKE PARTISAN GERRYMANDERING ILLEGAL," BY DAVID DALEY, FROM BILLMOYERS.COM, OCTOBER 2, 2017

JUSTICE ANTHONY KENNEDY COULD PROVIDE THE DECIDING VOTE IN GILL V. WHITFORD, AN UPCOMING CASE THAT LOOKS AT GERRYMANDERING IN WISCONSIN. ORAL ARGUMENTS BEGIN TUESDAY.

When the worst blizzard in 130 years pummeled Madison, Wisconsin in February 2011, something impossible happened: It stranded Green Bay Packers fans trying to travel to Texas for the Super Bowl.

But even a storm powerful enough to deter hardy crazies known for cheering shirtless in sub-zero temperatures could not stop one thing: Partisan gerrymandering.

That job now rests with one man: Supreme Court Justice Anthony Kennedy.

Kennedy will now scrutinize the constitutionality of the Wisconsin state assembly districts that the Republican operatives worked through a blizzard to craft. They delivered exactly as intended. In 2012, the first election held on these maps, Democratic candidates won 174,000 more votes. Republicans, nevertheless, won 60 of 99 seats.

That tilted outcome, however, launched the litigation that now provides the best hope in more than a decade of defeating gerrymandering — the toxic art of manipulating maps for partisan advantage — once and for all.

On Tuesday, the Supreme Court will hear oral arguments in *Gill v. Whitford*. The stakes could not be higher, or the court more closely divided. Kennedy, long alarmed by partisan gerrymandering but never convinced that there's a fair way to determine when it has gone too far, looks like the deciding vote.

It's a position he asked to be in, and a case he practically invited before the court. "Now we will see if Kennedy was being truthful," said Norm Ornstein, a resident scholar at the American Enterprise Institute. "He asked for a standard. The Wisconsin case provides a very clear example."

When the Supreme Court last addressed partisan gerrymandering, in the 2004 case *Vieth v. Jubelirer*, Kennedy sided with a 5-4 conservative majority that rejected an argument from Pennsylvania voters who claimed an aggressive GOP gerrymander interfered with their constitutional right to equal protection.

But while Justice Scalia and three other conservatives wanted to call partisan gerrymandering non-justiciable and slam the door on the court's involvement in future challenges, Kennedy kept it cracked, unprepared to declare that a fair standard could not someday emerge. Then he dropped breadcrumbs along the path reformers would need to follow to earn his backing next time.

It must be a "limited and precise rationale," based on a "clear, manageable and politically neutral standard" that shows partisanship was "applied in an invidious manner" or in such a way "unrelated to any legitimate legislative objective." Kennedy observed that while sophisticated new mapmaking software represented a potential threat to democracy, "these new technologies may produce new methods of analysis that make more evident the precise nature of the burdens gerrymanders impose on the representational rights of voters and parties." If so, he concluded, "courts should be prepared to order relief."

"The thing that I took away from the concurring opinion was that he believes that extreme partisan gerrymandering is unconstitutional, so long as we can come up with a standard," said Gerry Hebert, who argued and won the lower court cases in *Whitford*, and the executive director of the Campaign Legal Center. "Secondly, he expressed, the hope that there *would* someday be a standard."

The Wisconsin case hinges on a three-part test that convinced a lower court last year to declare the GOP maps unconstitutional. First, they presented evidence of discriminatory partisan intent, including dramatic emails between strategists declaring plans to "wildly gerry-mander" and dozens of draft maps with titles like "aggres-sive" and "assertive."

Then they developed a new standard called the "efficiency gap," which measures a partisan gerry-mander by counting the number of votes on both sides that do not contribute to victory. It helps demonstrate whether a party held an unfair advantage in converting votes into seats. When compared across states and over five decades, the Wisconsin gerrymander was one of the 18 worst in modern history.

"What I think we have here, for the first time, is a standard that can be applied by judges," said Hebert. "It's not difficult math. This is 6th grade math we're talking about here."

The final part of the standard considers whether there is a compelling justification for the districts being drawn in such a way — such as compliance with the Voting Rights Act, or holding communities of interest together.

While some of the faces have changed since *Vieth*, none of the four conservative justices, or the four liberals, seem likely to be moved. So what about Kennedy? Will the efficiency gap and these other measures be enough to bring about the first constitutional standard on partisan gerrymandering in our history, right on the eve of the 2020 midterms and the next round of redistricting? Longtime watchers are struggling to read his mind.

"It's not clear to me that the standards that are proposed are different in kind from what was already addressed in *Vieth*," said Richard L. Hasen, a professor of law and political science at the University of California, Irvine. "But there are two differences from then. One is that there now seems to be a scholarly near-consensus that it's possible to do a partisan gerrymander that lasts an entire decade, thanks to improvements in data and computer technology. That might weigh on Justice Kennedy. It imposed more of a hardship on voters."

The other difference: Kennedy's retirement appears close at hand. "This is set up as potentially the last big opportunity for him to do something about partisan gerrymandering. He's much more likely to do something than someone else that Trump might nominate. He has to know that."

Other scholars express some skepticism about whether the efficiency gap is actually the game-changing standard that some have suggested.

"This case looks pretty much like *Bandemer* and *Vieth*," said Bradley A. Smith, the former chairman of the Federal Election Commission and chairman of the conservative Center for Competitive Politics. "The efficiency gap doesn't add much to the analysis. Note that the lower court merely saw the 'gap' as evidence, not some new, killer theory."

Smith argues that Kennedy's position in *Vieth* remains about right: It's not wise to close the door on the possibility that a gerrymander could be unconstitutional, "but as a practical matter, that would be a rare case and very difficult to prove," he said. "There's no right to win political races, so unless a gerrymander really boxes out voters over time, it's not a constitutional problem. I don't think [*Whitford*] gets there. But what Kennedy thinks, I don't know. I don't see clues in his other writings."

Michael McDonald, however, a professor at the University of Florida and one of the nation's leading redistricting experts, pointed to Kennedy's decision in *Cooper v. Harris* as one potential signpost. In May, when the Court overturned two North Carolina congressional districts last month as an unconstitutional racial gerrymander, Kennedy disagreed and signed onto a dissent by Justice Samuel Alito that expressed concern about whether the Supreme Court ought to arbitrate partisan gerrymandering at all.

McDonald is also unconvinced that the efficiency gap necessarily meets Kennedy's call for a clear and manageable standard.

"The efficiency gap is fundamentally the same as every other measure that has been put before the court. Fundamentally it's about translating votes into seats and how well the system does that," he said. "Kennedy himself has been skeptical of these methods that have been put before him in amicus briefs.

"I just don't see it. There's no bright-line standard in the efficiency gap as to say when a redistricting plan is unconstitutional," he said, arguing that because election conditions and redistricting processes are variable across states, it's impossible to draw meaningful comparisons.

If the *Whitford* plaintiffs carry the day, McDonald said, it's could be because there have been multiple elections in Wisconsin with anti-majoritarian outcomes.

"By multiple measures — not just the efficiency gap — there's ample evidence to say 'this is a stacked system,'" he said. "I would hope that Kennedy would take a similar approach that is used in racial gerrymandering cases, look at all the evidence together, and let the courts come to a decision. I hope he will movie in that direction and articulate something in that way. But the efficiency gap alone, I fear, is not going to do it."

Hebert, however, maintains that the efficiency gap need not be a silver-bullet democracy theorem to carry the day, that Kennedy could simply view it as one useful tool among others. He also knows that time is running out, and that the replacement of Kennedy or any of the four liberal justices by President Trump could provide the fifth vote to make any future partisan gerrymandering cases non-justiciable for good.

"If we don't win this case, I don't have much hope that it will happen in my lifetime, if at all," Hebert said. "Kennedy would really be giving America the greatest gift. We've lost a lot of our democracy, and he would give it back to us. That would be an awesome thing to leave as a legacy for his time on his court."

1. The author discusses how the Supreme Court might decide this latest gerrymandering case after having determined in the past that there was no way to measure partisanship in redistricting. Do you think the arguments presented here are different from the arguments you've read about in previous cases?

CHAPTER 4

WHAT ADVOCACY ORGANIZATIONS SAY

The majority of the advocacy groups working on the issue of gerrymandering are opposed to the practice. They believe that gerrymandering devalues certain voters and causes elections to be won in an unfair manner. But what can or should be done to fix the problem is up for debate. In the following articles, you'll see what different anti-gerrymandering advocates feel is the real problem and how each proposes to solve it. As you read, consider how their arguments are similar, as well as how they're different, and which of their proposals is most likely to appeal to the legislators who draw the district maps.

"DRAINING THE SWAMP: A HOW-TO GUIDE," BY GARY D. BASS AND DANIELLE BRIAN, FROM *OTHERWORDS*, DECEMBER 14, 2016

IF TRUMP CARES ABOUT UNRIGGING THE SYSTEM LIKE HE'S SAID, HERE ARE FIVE THINGS HE CAN DO

When President-elect Donald Trump talked about "draining the swamp," it evoked the way Bernie Sanders talks about how the system is rigged. Many Americans believe — with good reason — that powerful corporate lobbyists, elites, and other moneyed interests control the levers of government.

Trump has pledged to refrain from nominating corporate lobbyists for political positions, to restrict appointees from lobbying for five years after leaving their government posts, and to do something about conflicts of interest arising from his own extensive business interests.

But in order to truly drain the swamp, he'll need to do far more. Here are five additional elements we hope Trump includes in his plan:

1. START WITH THE TOP.

Trump needs to turn over his family businesses into a true blind trust managed by an independent trustee with no ties to his family. The trustee should dispose of any business enterprises behind the blind trust wall and invest the new assets without any information going to Trump himself.

Cabinet appointees, too, need to be free of conflicts of interest in order to effectively serve the national interest.

2. CRACK DOWN ON POLITICAL APPOINTEES WITH FINANCIAL CONFLICTS.

Trump should issue an executive order on his first day in office cracking down not on lobbyists, but on all those with financial conflicts of interest. Focusing on lobbyists simply allows them to game the system by de-registering.

The executive order should also include restrictions on all political appointees from using government positions to curry favor with past and future employers.

That means there should be a ban on private gifts or compensation to people going into the administration. And appointees involved in policy decisions should be barred from working for any private entity that's materially benefited from those policies.

3. STOP THE MONEY GAME.

Along with money in politics, Trump needs to do something about what we call "money in policy." Between elections, billions of dollars are spent each year by powerful interests in order to influence policies, contracts, and other decisions at federal agencies. The next administration should limit this type of government capture.

Similarly, Trump should push for strict standards to keep special interests from dominating federal advisory committees tasked with making policy recommendations.

4. END THE SWEET DEALS FOR CONTRACTORS.

The incoming administration should reform and revamp the government's purchasing process to make it fair, transparent, and accountable to the public.

Under the current system, wealthy special interests are ripping off taxpayers by getting special access to lucrative government contracts. This pay-to-play system means average citizens and small businesses are not competing on a level playing field.

5. MAKE GOVERNMENT MORE OPEN AND PARTICIPATORY.

Trust in government, particularly in Congress, is practically nonexistent. One way to rebuild this trust is to engage the public, and not just powerful elites, in decision-making.

This starts with modernizing our voting systems to make it easier for every eligible person to cast a ballot. It also means putting an end to partisan and racial gerrymandering. At the same time, there needs to be greater transparency in government, more resources for oversight, and new ways to engage people in government decision-making.

"Swamp draining," however, is meaningless without a foundation in democratic values. All of the above efforts must be guided by protecting and advancing core principles of American democracy, such as a free press, an independent judiciary, and the constitutional presumption of equal protections under the law.

There are powerful moneyed interests with a stake in keeping the status quo. But President-elect Trump was voted into office by Americans who want change. A commitment to good government principles is essential to making that happen.

Danielle Brian is Executive Director of the Project On Government Oversight (POGO). Gary D. Bass is an affiliated professor at Georgetown University's McCourt School of Public Policy and founder of OMB Watch. Distributed by OtherWords.org.

1. The authors are both part of transparency-in-government organizations and they argue that ending gerrymandering starts with creating a more transparent government. Do you think transparency will help end the problem of gerrymandering? Why or why not?

2. Another problem discussed is money in politics and how it influences who has the power to redistrict and how that occurs. The authors here, as well as others in the book, believe that taking money out of politics is an important step in ending gerrymandering. In your own words, explain how this would help.

"THE VOTING RIGHTS ACT," BY MICAH ALTMAN AND MICHAEL MCDONALD, FROM THE PUBLIC MAPPING PROJECT

Short Definition: Under certain circumstances, minority opportunity districts must be drawn that have at least 50% minority voting-age population (VAP).

How to Determine Compliance in DistrictBuilder: DistrictBuilder's sidebar statistics include the number of minority opportunity districts in the plan used in the past decade and the number in the plan being drawn. Legal plans generally should have at least the same number of minority opportunity districts as the plan used for the past decade. If and when minority opportunity districts are proposed by a redistricting authority or other organization, such as the NAACP or MALDEF, we hope to make these districts available as a template from which software users can draw the remainder of a state.

The Voting Rights Act is an important federal redistricting requirement that ensures our representatives reflect America's racial and ethnic diversity. It enjoys overwhelming bipartisan congressional support. The U.S. Department of Justice and the NAACP Legal Defense Fund's Redrawing the Lines are excellent sources of information about the Voting Rights Act. Please bear in mind that the law regarding the Voting Rights Act is intricate and cannot possibly be covered in full depth here. Here are some of the important highlights.

WHY HAVE A VOTING RIGHTS ACT?

Following the Civil War, the United States adopted three important amendments to the U.S. constitution. Among these is the 15th Amendment, which states that "right of citizens of the United States to vote shall not be denied or abridged by the United States or by any state on account of race, color, or previous condition of servitude."

Immediately following the Civil War, the North occupied the South during a period known as Reconstruction. The North enforced the U.S. constitution, and as a result, many African-Americans were elected to state offices across the South. When the North withdrew its forces, White Southerners regained political power at first through violent intimidation during elections to repress African-American voting. Once in power, Whites amended their state constitutions and adopted election laws designed to prevent African-Americans from voting. Some of these rules may be familiar, such as the poll tax or discriminatory application of voter registration and literacy tests. A more obscure discriminatory device was racial gerrymandering.

The Voting Rights Act addressed all of these discriminatory election rules to ensure that our legislatures at all levels of government reflect the racial and ethnic diversity of the people they represent. Provisions of the Voting Rights Act have been amended and reauthorized several times to address changing legal and political environments. The most recent reauthorization for another twenty-five years passed by wide bipartisan margins in 2007 -- when Republicans controlled the U.S. Congress and George W. Bush was president. The Voting Rights Act is seen as one of the most successful pieces of legislation, being credited with the election of 9,000 African-Americans, 5,000 Latinos, and numerous Native Americans to local, state, and national offices.

The Voting Rights Act applies to redistricting to prevent states and localities from drawing districts that deny minorities a chance to elect a candidate of their choice. There are two important provisions. Section 2 applies nationally, and Section 5 applies only to certain "covered jurisdictions" which are located primarily in the South. These provisions are discussed in detail below. To understand how Section 2 and Section 5 apply, it is first important to understand how racial gerrymandering works.

WHAT IS RACIAL GERRYMANDERING?

To understand how to do a racial gerrymander, consider a hypothetical state with thirty-six people in it, which we will call Gerryland. Sixteen Gerrylanders are of a racial minority (represented by tan colored circles) and twenty are the racial majority. There are four districts to be drawn. (Thanks for Justin Levitt, formerly at the Brennan Center for Justice at New York University Law School, for these diagrams.)

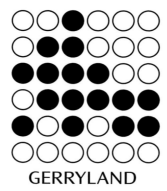

GERRYLAND

Racially polarized voting is when all the minorities always vote for their preferred candidate and all the majorities always vote for their preferred candidate. If racially polarized voting exists, it is possible to gerrymander with brutal efficiency to ensure minorities have little or no representation in a four-seat legislature. There are two gerrymandering strategies, known as cracking and packing. The same strategies apply to both racial and partisan gerrymandering.

Cracking is when the minority community is fragmented into several districts, none of which have a majority of minorities. When there is racially polarized voting, minorities will be unable to elect a candidate of their choice to the legislature in any district. The cracking strategy in Gerryland might look something like this.

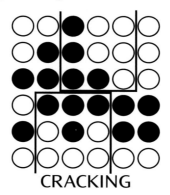

CRACKING

Stacking is when the minority community is concentrated into a small number of districts so that their votes are wasted in a district that their preferred candidate will win by an overwhelming margin. The packing strategy in Gerryland might look something like this, where the minority community is concentrated into one district.

PACKING

In practice, things are more complicated than the simple Gerryland example. Communities do not fit into nice squares, so the federal courts are fairly lenient on what minorities districts may look like. Some of the ugliest looking district ducklings are beautiful swans in the eyes of the courts. For example, the Illinois 4th Congressional District drawn in the 2000's decade is often called the "earmuff" district for obvious reasons. The western portion of this district actually travels along the northbound lane of Interstate 294! But, this district has a very important purpose. It was initially created in the 1990s to elect the first Latino representative to Congress from the Midwest.

The 4th congressional district has its funny shape because there is an African-American community sandwiched between two Latino communities. The African-American community is represented by the 7th Congressional district, which is designed to elect an African-American candidate of choice. The 4th district was wrapped around the 7th district so that both African-American and Latino communities could have congressional representation.

WHEN MUST A MINORITY OPPORTUNITY DISTRICT BE DRAWN?

The ideal district has just the right percentage of minorities to elect a minority candidate of choice. The percentage of minorities cannot be too low, lest cracking occurs, and cannot be too high, lest packing occurs. Determining the legally acceptable minority percentage requires the following steps:

1. First, perform a statistical analysis of election results to determine the degree of racially polarized voting.

2. Second, draw a district with enough minority population to elect a minority candidate of choice, given the statistical analysis.

The Supreme Court recently ruled in *Bartlett v Strickland* that in order for a district to be constitutionally required, minorities must constitute at least 50% of a minority opportunity district's voting-age population. Some have further interpreted this to mean that minorities must constitute at least 50% citizen voting-age population of a minority opportunity district. This is not to say that states cannot draw districts what are known as *influence districts*, where the minority community is a near majority, just that they are not required to do under federal law if they cannot draw a 50% district.

The most accessible population data to assess when a minority opportunity district must be drawn is voting-age population. The Census Bureau releases two types of data: total population, used to ensure districts are of equal population, and voting-age population, to ensure compliance with the Voting Rights Act. In the District-Builder software, we have made available the voting-age population data by race and ethnicity. (The issue of citizen-voting age population is a complicated one; more on this soon.)

There are two important sections of the Voting Rights Act that apply to the creation of minority opportunity districts, Section 2 and Section 5.

SECTION 2

Section 2 applies nationally. Essentially, Section 2 requires that if there is racially polarized voting and if a minority opportunity district can be drawn, then it must be drawn. (There is a further consideration, known as the "totality of the circumstances," which involves the history of past discrimination in the jurisdiction in question.)

SECTION 5

Section 5 applies only to covered jurisdictions. These jurisdictions must clear any electoral change--from moving a polling place to redistricting--with the

CRITICAL PERSPECTIVES ON GERRYMANDERING

Department of Justice or the District Court of DC before it can take effect. (The Department of Justice is the overwhelming pathway of choice.) This federal oversight is intended to ensure that a change does not have a discriminatory effect. In the context of redistricting, Section 5 requires that the number of minority opportunity districts cannot decrease during redistricting. This is called *retrogression*.

The Department of Justice has 60 days to review a redistricting plan to ensure compliance with Section 5. It may request another 60 days for additional review. If a redistricting plan is not cleared in a timely manner, or worse it is rejected and the state or locality has insufficient time to correct deficiencies, courts may impose their own plans for use in the next election. State law may allow or forbid a subsequent "re-redistricting." Because Section 5 only applies to covered jurisdictions, federal courts are not required to clear their plans before they take effect.

The Department of Justice has released "Guidance Concerning Redistricting Under Section 5 of the Voting Rights Act." To underscore the importance of the Public Mapping Project to minority voting interests, the Department of Justice states

> In considering whether less-retrogressive alternative plans are available, the Department of Justice looks to plans that were actually considered or drawn by the submitting jurisdiction, as well as alternative plans presented or made known to the submitting jurisdiction by interested citizens or others.

Thus, plans drawn by the public may factor into the Department of Justice's decision to approve a redistricting plan submitted by a covered jurisdiction.

WHAT IS REQUIRED IN PRACTICE

In practice, Section 2 and Section 5 essentially require that at least the same number of minority opportunity districts in a previous redistricting plan must be drawn in a new redistricting plan. Section 5 explicitly requires this, and Section 2 has been litigated in most parts of the country. There are two exceptions:

1. In areas where minority populations have grown, such as Latino communities in Texas, more minority opportunity districts may be required under Section 2. The Supreme Court has ruled that it is permissible for states and localities to draw such districts to avoid litigation.

2. In areas where minority populations have decreased, it may be impossible to draw a minority opportunity district. In this case, a minority opportunity district may not be required.

   How and where minority opportunity districts must be drawn will not become clear until racial polarization analyses are conducted, districts are draw, and in certain circumstance, the Department of Justice and the courts review the evidence.

It is beyond the capabilities of most ordinary citizens -- and sometimes even redistricting authorities! -- to comply with all the intricacies of the Voting Rights Act. To provide clues as to whether or not your districts are in compliance, on the statistics sidebar on the righthand side of the plan editor, we report the number of districts with more than 50% minority voting-age population (VAP) in the plan used for the previous decade and the number in the plan you are drawing. Typically, you should have at least the same number in your plan as in the previous plan.

1. The authors discuss the many ways that districts are gerrymandered. Explain each of the ways—cracking, stacking, and packing—in your own terms.

2. Sometimes redistricting is required because of changes in the population. From this article, what are some instances when new districts need to be drawn? How are the new districts determined?

"FUNNY SHAPES AREN'T THE PROBLEM WITH AMERICAN VOTING," BY LEE DRUTMAN, FROM *NEW AMERICA*, FEBRUARY 11, 2016

In his final State of the Union address, President Obama had a few words on how we ought to change the political system. First on his list? Gerrymandering. Here's what he said: "We have to end the practice of drawing our congressional districts so that politicians can pick their voters, and not the other way around."

This point has become almost de rigueur when listing the ills of American democracy, especially among Democrats who feel that Republicans have drawn district maps to give them an unfair advantage in the U.S. House. (Obama mentioned it again in a speech in Illinois just yesterday.)

And the solution seems so simple: Why can't we just have independent, nonpartisan districting commissions who can take the politics out of line drawing?

If only it really were so simple.

Really, the bigger problem here is with the single-member, winner-take-all congressional district. But before I get to that problem, let's understand why gerrymandering is not quite the evil it's made out to be, and why redistricting reform is not quite the cure-all.

Generally, there are three objections to gerrymandering:

1. It creates ugly-looking districts

2. It reduces competition

3. Parties draw the map to unfairly benefit them

UGLY-LOOKING DISTRICTS

Yes, state redistricting commissions draw some ugly looking districts. But then again, so does Mother Nature. Consider the state of Rhode Island.

Certainly, you can get a computer to make many districts that look more compact than they currently do. But why should we prize aesthetics in congressional districting? This is an entirely arbitrary standard that has nothing to say about either competition or congruence with actual communities.

In fact, some of the most often ridiculed districts were drawn by public interest-groups upholding goals of minority representation enshrined in the Voting Rights Act.

THE DECLINE OF COMPETITIVE DISTRICTS

A more widespread objection to redistricting is the claim that gerrymandering has reduced competition in American congressional elections.

Certainly, fewer and fewer House elections are contested. By the latest estimates of the Cook Political Report, only 16 (out of 435) House Seats are considered toss-ups. Most House seats are pretty solidly safe for one party or the other.

But is this because of gerrymandering?

It's possible that a few states have made some seats less competitive through their redistricting processes. But the reason that most seats are not competitive anymore has far more to do with the geographical sorting of the two parties.

Consider the state of Washington. Here are the presidential results from 2012. [*Editor's note: Maps are not included here and can be found in the original publication.*]

The urban areas on the coast are solidly Democratic. The rural areas inland are solidly Republican. If map-drawers wanted to draw districts to maximize competition, perhaps they could find a way to split the state into ten horizontal bars. But inland and coastal Washington are very different places. To the extent that we want representatives who have some connection to the place they represent, this would be a very dumb idea.

Washington State is not an outlier, just a clear example. In general, urban areas are solidly Democratic; suburban and rural areas are solidly Republican. This poses serious problems for electoral competition.

This decline in competition didn't happen because of gerrymandering. It happened because the two parties became more clearly sorted, both ideologically and geographically. And as a result, both swing voting and split-ticket voting have declined considerably. In many states, there's just no way to draw many competitive districts without drawing many skinny rectangles.

This geographical problem winds up to be particularly problematic for Democrats, who over-concentrate their voters in urban areas, giving Democrats more 80+% Democratic districts. By comparison, Republican voters control more 60-70% Republican districts. Because Republican voters are spread out a little better across more districts, this means they can win more Congressional seats.

PARTIES DRAW THE MAP TO UNFAIRLY BENEFIT THEM

In partisan redistricting, the goal is to get the most seats. That means making the most economical use of your voters, trying to spread them as widely as possible. Certainly, both parties do this.

But both because Republicans control more state legislatures now and because of the geography of Republican voting (remember, Republican voters are more evenly distributed geographically), Republicans have more successfully drawn themselves more seats than they would under a proportional representation direct translation of votes to seats.

Political scientist Nicholas Goedert has found that in Republican gerrymandered states, Republicans outperform their expected share of seats by 19 percentage points, whereas Democrats outperform their expected share of seats by only five percentage points.

But there is an upside to partisan gerrymandering—it makes seats more competitive than they would otherwise be. Since the goal of partisan gerrymandering is to spread out your party's voters more evenly, this produces more competitive districts.

THE PROBLEM IS SINGLE-MEMBER WINNER-TAKE-ALL DISTRICTS

In drawing district lines, there are many trade-offs. It's really hard to have districts that are both compact and competitive. Partisan redistricting generally makes districts more competitive than they would otherwise be, but this hardly absolves partisan redistricting of other distortions.

Ultimately, though, competition has to be the biggest concern. Absent competitive districts, the parties will have little incentive to move to their middle and so will move to their extremes, particularly as their geographical centers of power grow further apart. And this increasing partisan-geography division in turn makes it really hard to draw competitive districts—a particularly difficult loop.

The only way we'll solve this problem in the current partisan polarization is to get rid of the single-member district, and move to multi-member districts.

Reihan Salam once called the single-member district "The Biggest Problem in American Politics." Salam is a conservative living in liberal Brooklyn. Under single-member winner-take-all systems, he will never be represented by a Republican. But if five New York City districts merged into one in order to elect five members, a Republican could plausibly get elected to represent the 20% or so New York City Republicans. That New York City

Republican would also be a different kind of Republican than a Republican from Texas or Alabama, creating more diversity within the Republican Party.

Magnify this across the country, and you'd get more electoral competition, and more diversity within the parties, particularly if you add in ranked-choice voting. And no more worrying about gerrymandering. To understand better how this would all work, I recommend checking the website of FairVote, which has been a leading advocate for proportional representation and multi-member districts.

Certainly, it's easy to complain about the process of gerrymandering, in part because the solution seems so simple—just take it out of the hands of politicians. But the real problem here is not that districts have funny shapes. The real problem is that voters are sorted by partisanship and geography in ways that makes it hard to draw competitive single-member districts. And to solve that problem, we're going to need to get more creative.

1. The author discusses how Democrats and Republicans tend to move to areas where they are likely to find more people like themselves, with Democrats making up a large majority of urban areas while Republicans spread out more. Do you think this is a reason for districts to be redrawn?

2. There is an upside to gerrymandering according to the author—it creates more competitive races

for congressional seats. Do you think this is a good reason to allow parties to continue to redraw the voting districts to their liking?

"REDISTRICTING IN COLORADO: CLEARING HURDLES, LOOMING COURT FIGHT, PICK UPS AND PUTDOWNS," BY COREY HUTCHINS, FROM *THE COLORADO INDEPENDENT*, DECEMBER 8, 2017

A bipartisan group seeking to change the way Colorado draws its political boundaries has moved one step closer to its goal — and toward a likely battle before the state's highest court.

Fair Districts Colorado can begin gathering voter signatures to put its redistricting measures on the 2018 ballot, a state panel ruled Wednesday. It's the latest hurdle cleared by a group of political heavyweights who say they want to take partisanship out of the once-every-10-years redistricting process.

At stake is the balance of power in Colorado for decades to come. The statehouse is currently split with Republicans holding a one-seat majority in the Senate and Democrats controlling the House by several. How district lines are drawn can make winning for one party easier or harder, and over the years the process in Colorado has led to bitter court fights and bruising battles between the state's two largest political parties.

In Colorado, the legislature currently carves up the districts represented by the state's seven members of Congress. An 11-member panel of Republicans and Democrats chosen by the governor, Supreme Court Justice, and legislative leaders approves the districts for members of the state legislature.

Fair Districts wants to change that. Part of its plan calls for a more independent 12-member commission made up of four Democrats, four Republicans, and four people not affiliated with a major political party to approve district lines for the legislature. A similar commission would do the same for Congress. The idea is to have more representation in the process for voters in Colorado who choose to remain independent from a political party. Unaffiliated voters here make up the state's largest voting population.

The push in Colorado comes as similar proposals are popping up nationwide and as the U.S. Supreme Court considers the question of whether partisan gerrymandering— the practice of drawing political lines to favor one political party over another— is constitutional.

But a resistance movement against the plan is also gathering.

On Dec. 6, Denver elections attorney Mark Grueskin, who has represented Democrats in previous redistricting battles, unsuccessfully argued to the state Title Board, which approves ballot measure language, that Fair Districts shouldn't be able to move forward with gathering signatures. He is concerned language in the plan isn't simpatico with the group's stated purpose of trying to create more competitive districts. If Fair Districts is successful, Grueskin worries race could become a basis for district line-drawing, which he says would be a "radical departure" from the way redistricting has been done in Colorado. Attorney Bill Hobbs, arguing for Fair Districts, says that's the opposite of the group's intent.

Grueskin says he will appeal the Title Board's ruling to the state Supreme Court and make his argument there. It could take months to resolve, and before that Fair Districts is unlikely to begin trying to gather signatures, Hobbs says. Grueskin, meanwhile, teased the possibility that a different group in Colorado might put forward a counterproposal to compete with the Fair Districts plan. He declined to discuss details.

Following the Title Board hearing, Common Cause of Colorado came out against the Fair Districts campaign.

The state group, whose national chapter keeps an eye on redistricting around the country, doesn't like that the Fair District's proposal calls for partisan politicians to appoint most of the redistricting commissioners— which is also how it works now— among other issues involving transparency and scant buy-in from minority communities.

"While the measures do include a more neutral selection process for the unaffiliated or independent members, that change is not enough to eliminate the overall partisan selection process of the majority of the members," Common Cause Colorado wrote in a statement.

Hobbs called the elections watchdog group's opposition disappointing because he says Fair Districts engaged with Common Cause and incorporated some of its suggestions into the plan. "We really tried to incorporate their concerns and unfortunately they still are not on board," he says. "Everything that we're doing is an improvement on the current process."

Debates about partisanship have dogged the Fair Districts campaign from its start.

An early version of its plan allowed the state's two largest political parties to choose a majority of the members on the proposed new independent redistricting commission. Critics, like Grueskin, worried doing so would actually increase partisanship. Political parties are accountable to party insiders while elected officials are accountable to voters, he said. Fair Districts later changed course and gave the appointing power to legislative leaders.

Fair Districts also came in for criticism for not having enough buy-in from minority groups, though the group said it made a good-faith effort in its outreach. Since the group launched, two prominent Latino Democrats, former Lt. Gov. Joe Garcia and ex-lawmaker Abel Tapia, pulled their support from the plan. Garcia said the Fair Districts campaign and its efforts are "more controversial and potentially partisan" than he realized.

Along the way, the backgrounds of some involved in the effort have also drawn scrutiny.

Last year, a group called End Gerrymandering Now tried unsuccessfully to put a similar redistricting proposal on the ballot but was blocked on a technicality by the state supreme court. Its backers included former GOP House Speaker Frank McNulty and former GOP Senate Minority Leader Josh Penry, Republican redistricting operative Alan Philp as well as former Democratic Secretary of State Bernie Buescher, PR consultant Rich Coolidge, and

Kathleen Curry, a one-time Democratic lawmaker who later became unaffiliated. All of them are working on this year's Fair Districts Colorado proposal.

In response to early criticism, Fair Districts made some other changes to its proposal between the time the campaign launched in September and this week's Title Board hearing. Beyond the change to give appointing power to lawmakers instead of parties, having the non-major party members of the commissions ultimately chosen by a random lottery after screening by retired judges instead of whittled down by partisans as the group initially proposed, was an additional tweak to the plan.

Another change this year is the support Fair Districts counts from wealthy powerbroker Kent Thiry, the CEO of the Denver-based kidney dialysis company DaVita. In recent years, Thiry has positioned himself as an advocate for Colorado's 1.3 million unaffiliated voters. Last year he backed a successful statewide ballot measure that allows unaffiliated voters to participate in party primaries.

In another big move, Fair Districts gained the backing of the League of Women Voters of Colorado, though that wasn't without drama. A split among leadership over whether to support the plan ended with the departure of the group's president, Nancy Crow.

"The fallout was I resigned from the board," Crow told *The Colorado Independent* this week. "I lost support." She says she feels strongly that the League is being used to lend credibility to a redistricting plan she worries could be part of a national strategy to turn more state legislatures red.

The state League's new president is Toni Larson, who has been working with the Fair Districts campaign for nearly a year. On Dec. 7, the state League's board voted to fully support the Fair Districts plan, she says, and to encourage its local chapters to help gather signatures for it if and when they are able.

Says Larson: "We have decided that we are thoroughly behind Fair Districts Colorado."

1. In Colorado, an activist group is trying to get a non-partisan commission approved to handle all future redistricting to avoid partisan gerrymandering. Do you think such a commission is possible? Explain why or why not.

2. A different group mentioned in the article believes it's a problem for partisan politicians to appoint the members of the redistricting commission, even if the commission does have an even mix of members from both parties. Do you agree with their assessment? How would you appoint members to a non-partisan redistricting team?

CHAPTER 5

WHAT THE
MEDIA SAY

L ike advocacy groups, most in the media believe that gerrymandering is a problem that negatively affects American democracy. But how that happens and why is up for discussion in the press. Some believe that it's a big problem that impacted the last presidential election, while others in the media see it as a smaller, more ongoing issue that has its biggest toll on local elections. Whatever the case, the media has a lot to say about their side, and you'll read a number of takes in this chapter from members of the press.

"THE REAL WAY THE 2016 ELECTION IS RIGGED," BY DAVID DALEY, FROM BILLMOYERS.COM *AT COMMON DREAMS*, AUGUST 21, 2016

Hillary Clinton has put the Electoral College into check-mate. She's closer to Donald Trump in many red states like Kansas and Texas than he is to her in key swing states.

As her lead swells, naturally, fired-up Democrats and a restless media have turned their attention to a more exciting story: Can Democrats retake the House of Representatives? But the outcome there is not really in doubt, either.

It's not going to happen. Democratic House candidates will likely get many more votes than Republican ones – as they did in 2012, when Democrats received 1.4 million more votes nationwide, but Republicans maintained a 234-201 advantage. Indeed, Trump is more likely to rebound in swing states than Democrats are to capture the 30 congressional seats they need to pry the speaker's gavel from Paul Ryan.

Even if Hillary Clinton wins the presidency in a landslide, there are simply not enough competitive districts remaining to give the Democrats any chance at winning the House. The reason why is simple, structural and too often absent from the conversation: It's the radical GOP gerrymander imposed after the 2010 census on purplish states like Pennsylvania, Ohio, Michigan, Wisconsin and North Carolina – all of which are likely to go for Clinton, while also electing a bright-red Republican delegation to Congress. Even if

For all of the misleading nonsense about "rigged elections" coming from the Trump camp this summer, we haven't talked enough about the way our electoral map really was rigged by Republicans after the 2010 census. These tilted maps make it possible for the Republicans to govern with a supermajority in Ohio, North Carolina and Wisconsin – despite getting less votes overall. And they've created a firewall in the House of Representatives that's built to withstand a Clinton landslide upward of 10 percent.

LIES OF OMISSION

Democrats, however, prefer to raise false hopes — and raise money — by pretending the House is in play. The media, desperate for any suspenseful narrative, pretends that gerrymandering is politics as usual and that both sides do it — stubbornly refusing to understand how the brazen and technologically savvy 2011 remapping was different from any other in modern political history. *The New York Times*, earlier this month in a story headlined "How House Republicans May Survive Donald Trump," cast this in a bizarrely passive voice – "House Republicans have strong defenses in the congressional district boundaries, which set the terms of competition" – without mentioning how Republicans drew most of these lines themselves.

Then on Friday, the *Times* continued to fuel the debate with a Page One story with the opposite headline – "Republicans Worry a Falling Donald Trump Tide Will Lower All Boats" – had the same view from nowhere. It observed that "so many districts are drawn to make them uncompetitive in general election," as if they were drawn by magic or drew themselves, never bothering to note who drew them that way, and the multimillion dollar GOP project to ensure some 400 of 435 House elections were uncompetitive. (It also quotes Pennsylvania congressman Charlie Dent, wringing his hands. "We have to be concerned," said the Republican congressman whose new can't-lose district shed Democratic towns after 2011 and took on the shape of a bad toupee in a windstorm. "I don't think you can assume anybody is safe." But that Dent himself is unbeatable goes without saying in the *Times* piece. His "chopped-up mess" of a district in the words of the *Lehigh Valley Express-Times*, is so GOP-friendly that no Democrat would oppose him in 2014.)

The New York Times has managed the amazing trick of writing multiple stories across months about the likelihood of a Democratic House takeover without even using the word "gerrymander."

Instead, these stories, and others like them, tell anecdotal stories of districts that just might be in play. Indeed, one or two of them may be! For example, when conservative talk-radio host Jason Lewis captured a four-way fight for the GOP nomination for Congress in the purplish suburbs of Minneapolis and St. Paul earlier this month, giddy Democrats slid the open 2nd district seat into their column.

The first rule of journalism these days is that whenever a headline poses a question, the answer is no. In this case, it's hell no.

Lewis, a frequent fill-in for Rush Limbaugh, might be a master performance artist on air but figures to be a divisive fit for one of the country's last remaining swing districts. His book on states' rights, after all, manages to suggest that if same-sex marriage is legal, slavery should be too. "People always say, 'Well, if you don't want to marry somebody of the same sex you don't have to, but why tell somebody else they can't,'" he argues. "Uh, you know, if you don't want to own a slave, don't. But don't tell other people they can't."

So that just might be one for the Democrats, especially since they're running a well-funded centrist businesswoman. Trouble is: It's just one, and the Republican advantage in the House is 247-188 — the GOP's biggest margin since Election Day 1928. Democrats still need 29 more.

For those seats, the political writers at *The New York Times* and McClatchy looked to Kansas's 3rd district after a Survey USA poll earlier this month found Hillary Clinton with a surprising lead there. (In contrast, Barack Obama only received 44 percent that district in in 2012.) "Could super-red Kansas elect a Democrat to Congress?" the breathless McClatchy headline asked. The first rule of journalism these days is that whenever a headline poses a question, the answer is no. In this case, it's hell, no. Despite the good polling numbers for Clinton, Republican incumbent Kevin Yoder leads Democratic challenger Jay Sidie 53 percent to 36 percent, according to an August poll from Public Opinion Strategies.

When you see stories like this, do the math yourself and ask exactly where these 30 Democratic victories will come. The vague and intentionally non-specific "suburban districts where educated Republicans are fleeing Trump" is not a sufficient answer. For some actual facts about actual districts, Larry Sabato's Crystal Ball Report examines conditions on the ground in all 435 districts. Last week, Sabato did move four races in the Democrats' direction — including Minnesota's 2nd and Kansas's 3rd. Yes, this means that in one of the four House races now considered potentially in play, the Republican holds a 17-point lead. That alone should be a sign of how daunting the math is for the Democrats.

But if that's not enough, try these numbers. Sabato already has called 226 seats as safe, likely or leaning to the Republicans, and just 193 as safe, likely or leaning to the Democrats. It only requires 218 to hold the chamber, so the Republicans need only win the seats they have overwhelming leads in now — at the likely peak of their presidential candidate's meltdown — to take the House. Let's pause for a second: That number alone ought to stop every think piece about whether the Democrats can win the House dead in its tracks.

If that doesn't convince you, here are some more powerful numbers: if the Republicans are heavily favored in 226 districts, and the Democrats look likely in 193, that only leaves a handful of toss-ups. Sabato sees 16 legitimate toss-ups. The problem for Democrats? Fourteen of those 16 seats are currently held by Republicans. In the highly unlikely circumstance that the Democrats manage to take just half of those 16 remaining "toss-up" seats, the Republicans would come out of 2016 with a 234-201 advantage in Congress.

If that sounds familiar, it should: 234-201 is the exact majority the Republicans had after 2012, when Barack Obama won re-election in a landslide but failed to take the House despite those 1.4 million more votes. That was the first time since 1972 — 40 years — that the party with the most votes did not come away with the most seats. It is now likely to happen again in 2016, for the second presidential cycle in a row. This should terrify anyone who cares about representative democracy. This is not politics as usual.

Few of these numbers matter to the pundit class. They'd rather talk about split tickets! We don't do that anymore! No one votes for one party for president and the other party for Congress. This has the benefit of being true, but also missing the point entirely. Because of the way congressional districts were drawn after 2011, a majority of voters can cast a straight-ticket ballot and it still won't change the Republican dominance of the House. In 2012 — when fewer voters split tickets than in any election in almost 100 years — Mitt Romney lost the election by 3.5 million votes and by an Electoral College margin of 332-206. Nevertheless: Romney still carried 226 congressional districts to Obama's 209. In Pennsylvania, for example, Obama carried the state for the second time. But Romney won 13 of the 18 congressional districts — and nine by near double-digits. That's the math Democrats have to defeat — lines that were drawn to push back any blue avalanche.

The credulous pundits who argue that Democrats could carry the House this year because voters no longer split tickets are grasping at straws. It takes no imagination at all to conjure suburban Republican voters in northern Virginia, Denver, Pennsylvania and elsewhere who believe Trump is a line too far — but who also cringe at the idea of giving Clinton a blank check in the House. Republican leaders and financiers are already planning on siphoning money away from Trump and using exactly this line to defend Congress.

Polls suggest that it will work: Real Clear Politics aggregates surveys that ask voters whether they want the Democrats or Republicans to control Congress. On this generic congressional ballot, the Democrats only lead by 5 points. In contrast, in June 2008, the last time the Democrats won the House, the Democrats held a 53-38 advantage on this question in an NBC poll.

Could a miracle happen? Sure. But it's high time that we're honest about what that miracle would look like. Democrats would have to win all 16 of the remaining toss-ups – 87 percent of which are currently held by Republicans. Then they would have to reverse 20-point deficits in several other districts to even get close.

This is not an accident. Chris Jankowski, who directed the audacious REDMAP strategy that delivered the GOP control of the House for this entire decade, if not longer, told me that he raised the necessary money in 2010 by telling Republican donors that they would save them money – and take expensive, competitive seats off the table for 10 years. "There are 25 true swing congressional districts," he said. "We found that $115 million had been spent on those 25 [from 2002-2008]. We had a graphic on the screen: $115 million hard dollars or $20 million in soft and we can fix it. We can take control of these 25 districts. We can take them off the table."

That's exactly what happened – and it's why the Republicans will control the House come January, no matter how big the Democrats win this fall, or how many times the topic gets debated on "Morning Joe" or in *The New York Times*. The media does our democracy a disservice by treating this like a true contest, and not being honest about the way one side tilted our democracy so that they could govern with fewer votes.

1. The author blames the media, in part, for making gerrymandering seem normal and acceptable. After reading the other articles in this and the following section, do you think the media's reporting on gerrymandering needs to change? If so, how?

2. Take one of the articles in this book and pick out three things that are done well in the reporting of a redistricting and three things that could have been written differently. How do you think the article you chose impacted readers as it was written? How would your edits change how the issue was viewed?

"AMERICA'S LONG (AND UNFINISHED) ROAD TO DEMOCRACY," BY DAVID MORRIS, FROM *COMMONS MAGAZINE*, NOVEMBER 12, 2016

SOME HISTORICAL CONTEXT ON US ELECTIONS

The founding fathers minced no words about their distrust of the masses. Our second President, John Adams warned, "Democracy will soon degenerate into an anarchy..." Our third President, Thomas Jefferson insisted, "Democracy is nothing more than mob rule." Our fourth President, James Madison, the Father of the Constitution declared, "Democracy is the most vile form of government."

In his argument against the direct election of Senators Connecticut's Roger Sherman advised his colleagues at the Constitutional Convention, "The people should have as little to do as may be about the government. They lack information and are constantly liable to be misled." They agreed. Senators would be elected by state legislatures. And they created the Electoral College to shield the Presidency from a direct vote of the people as well.

In 1776, the year he signed the Declaration of Independence, John Adams presciently wrote a fellow lawyer about the collateral damage that would result from "attempting to alter the qualifications of voters. There will be no end to it. New claims will arise. Women will demand the vote. Lads from 12 to 21 will think their rights not enough attended to, and every man who has not a farthing, will demand an equal voice with any other, in all acts of state. It tends to confound and destroy all distinctions, and prostrate all ranks to one common level."

In 1789 the franchise was restricted to white men, but not all white men. Only those possessing a minimum amount of property or paid taxes could vote. In 1800, just three states permitted white manhood suffrage–the right to vote–without qualification.

In 1812, six western states were the first to give all non-property owning white men the franchise. Hard times resulting from the Panic of 1819 led many people to demand an end to property restrictions on voting and officeholding. By 1840 popular agitation by the swelling ranks of propertyless urban dwellers coupled with "Age of Jacksonian Democracy" increased the percentage of white men eligible to vote to 90 percent. And the advent of a new type of presidential electioneering that spoke directly to the people in raucous proceedings lifted turnout from 25 percent of eligible voters in 1824 to a remarkable 80 percent in 1840.

Women had to wait much longer. A number of colonies did allow women to vote. But by the time the Constitution was ratified all states except New Jersey denied women that right. In 1808 New Jersey made it unanimous.

In 1860 Wyoming territory granted women the right to vote. In 1875 Michigan and Minnesota allowed women to vote for school boards. In 1887 Kansas gave them the right to vote in municipal elections. In 1889 Wyoming and Utah became the first states to grant women full suffrage. By 1920, the year the 19th Amendment was ratified women had achieved suffrage in 19 of the then 48 states.

BLACK SUFFRAGE

For blacks the road was much, much longer and far more treacherous. Even as the states extended voting rights to all white men it took away existing voting rights to black men. In the 1790s, African American males who owned property could vote in New York, Pennsylvania, Connecticut, Massachusetts, New Hampshire, Vermont, Maine, North Carolina, Tennessee, and Maryland. All effectively stripped their black citizens of voting rights in the first quarter of the 19th century.

Every new state that joined the Union after 1819 explicitly denied blacks the right to vote. Northern states were almost as averse as Southern states to black suffrage. As late as the end of the Civil War, 19 of 24 Northern states still refused to allow blacks the vote. In October 1865, five months after Appomattox the white men in Connecticut rejected a state constitutional amendment extending the right to vote to black men.

In 1860 Abraham Lincoln won only 40 percent of the vote. The majority, perhaps the vast majority, of Americans did not favor freeing the slaves. Indeed, on March 4, 1861, with the support of the President, Congress sent to the states a Constitutional Amendment that declared, "No amendment shall be made to the Constitution which will authorize or give to Congress the power to abolish or interfere, within any State, with the domestic institutions thereof, including that of persons held to labor or service by the laws of said State."

Three states had ratified the Amendment before the attack on Fort Sumter shifted the course of history.

"By the irony of fate, not the deliberate choice of men, the Thirteenth Amendment to the Constitution when it finally came was to abolish slavery in the United States, not to fasten it upon the continent to the end of time," historians Charles and Mary Beard mused.

In 1865, at a cost of more than 600,000 lives (half of all Americans killed in all wars) the 13th Amendment was ratified. It ended slavery but did not guarantee blacks civil rights nor the right to vote. The former Confederate states immediately enacted black codes that denied blacks basic civil rights, such as the right to serve on juries and testify against whites. In response Congress enacted, over President Andrew Johnson's veto, the Civil Rights Act of 1866 that demanded for blacks "full and equal benefit of all laws and proceedings for the security of person and property, as is enjoyed by white citizens, and shall be subject to like punishment, pains, and penalties, and to none other..." The Act also provided that federal rather than state courts would be the venue for litigation concerning the civil rights of the ex-slaves.

To make this extension of rights immune from future Congressional backsliding Congress submitted to the states the 14th Amendment which extended citizenship to "all persons born or naturalized in the United States" and forbidding states from denying any person "life, liberty or property, without due process of law" and "equal protection of the laws." The Amendment was ratified in 1868 after Congress demanded ratification as a precondition for southern states to regain representation.

The 14th Amendment, like the 13th Amendment, did not give blacks the right to vote. Instead it threatened to penalize states that did not. If the right to vote "is denied to any of the male inhabitants of such State, being twenty-one years of age, and citizens of the United States, or in any way abridged, except for participation in rebellion, or other crime, the basis of representation therein shall be reduced..."

The threat had no effect. The 15th Amendment finally granted blacks the right to vote. But as historian William Gillette observed, "It was hard going and the outcome was uncertain until the very end." Ratification passed by a paper-thin margin only because Congress continued to deny Virginia, Mississippi, Texas and Georgia Congressional representation until they voted in favor.

Ratified in February 1870 the 15th Amendment almost immediately gave rise to paramilitary groups like the Ku Klux Klan that intimidated black men who tried to exercise their newly won franchise. Congress again responded by passing Enforcement Acts in 1870 and 1871, sometimes called the Ku Klux Klan Acts. These established penalties for interfering with a person's right to vote and gave federal courts the power to enforce the Act. They also authorized the President to employ the army and use federal marshals to bring charges against offenders.

Violence against blacks continued. In 1872, a hotly disputed Louisiana election resulted in a federal judge ruling that the Republican Party, the party of Abraham Lincoln, won the legislature. Southern Democrats refused to accept that verdict. On April 13, 1873, an armed militia of white Democrats attacked black Republican freedmen massacring 105 black people. Federal prosecutors indicted three attackers.

The case went to the Supreme Court. The Court ruled that the due process and equal protection clauses of the 14h Amendment applied only to state action, and not to actions of individuals: "The fourteenth amendment prohibits a State from depriving any person of life, liberty, or property, without due process of law; but this adds nothing to the rights of one citizen as against another." The indictments were overturned.

Despite physical threats, blacks vigorously exercised their right to vote as long as federal troops protected that right. During the 1870s, more than a half-million black men in the South became voters. When Mississippi rejoined the Union in 1870, former slaves made up more than half of that state's population. During the next decade, Mississippi sent two black U.S. senators to Washington and elected a number of black state officials, including a lieutenant governor. (Interestingly, as the Constitutional Rights Foundation observes, "even though the new black citizens voted freely and in large numbers, whites were still elected to a large majority of state and local offices.") Texas elected 42 blacks to the State Legislature, South Carolina 50, Louisiana 127 and Alabama 99. The number of black state and federal legislators in the South peaked in 1872 at about 320 –a level that remains unsurpassed to this day.

These legislatures moved quickly to protect voting rights for blacks, prohibit segregation in public transportation and open juries to blacks. They also made major contributions to the welfare of poor whites as well as blacks by establishing the South's first systems of free public education, repealing imprisonment-for-debt laws, and abolishing property qualifications for holding office.

One would think the language of the 15th Amendment could not be clearer: "The right of citizens of the United States to vote shall not be denied or abridged by the United States or by any State on account of race, color, or previous condition of servitude." The Supreme Court saw it differently. In 1875 the high Court asserted, "The Fifteenth Amendment does not confer the right of suffrage upon anyone." States retained the right to establish "race-neutral" limitations on suffrage. These included poll taxes and literacy tests and even clauses that exempted citizens from these voting requirements if their grandfathers had been registered voters!

In 1877 the last of the Union troops were withdrawn. Southern legislatures ferociously stripped blacks of their hard-earned voting rights and liberties. Using poll taxes, literacy tests, physical intimidation and white only primaries Mississippi slashed the percentage of black voting-age men registered to vote from more than 90 percent to less than 6 percent in 1892. In Louisiana, the number of black registered voters plummeted from 130,000 to 1,342.

As late as 1940 a mere 3 percent of voting-age black men and women in the South were registered to vote. In Mississippi, that number was less than 1 percent. In 1963, only 156 of 15,000 eligible black voters in Selma, Alabama, were registered to vote. Between 1963 and 1965 the federal government filed four lawsuits but the number of black registered voters only increased from 156 to 383 during that time.

In 1964 the 24th Amendment prohibited poll taxes in federal elections. At the time, five Southern states still imposed that election requirement.

One might accurately say that only in 1965, a century after the Civil War ended did blacks effectively gain the right to vote. The Voting Rights Act sent federal examiners to seven Southern states to help register black voters and required states with a history of voter discrimination to gain pre-approval from the federal government before changing any voting requirements.

Within a year, 450,000 Southern blacks had registered to vote, about the same number that had voted in the South a century before. Recently African-American voter turnout has exceeded white turnout in all of the states originally covered by the Act.

While Congress extended the right to vote, the Supreme Court tried to make the value of each vote equal. In the 20th century states dominated by legislators elected from rural districts refused to reapportion their legislative districts despite the clear shift of populations to urban areas. The result was that in Alabama some districts with the same number of representatives were more than 40 times the population size of others. The vote of one Californian was worth as much as 422 times the vote of another.

Until 1962 the Supreme Court viewed gross electoral inequities as an internal state political matter immune from federal judicial intervention. That year it reversed itself. Two years later the Supreme Court affirmed and extended the 1962 decision in a case where Chief Justice Warren famously declared, "Legislators represent people, not trees or acres." States were ordered to reapportion their legislative districts every ten years and keep voting district populations more or less equal. The Court also upheld lower courts imposing temporary reapportionment when state legislatures proved recalcitrant.

On March 23, 1971, the 26th Amendment dropped the voting age from 21 to 18. The last of John Adam's dystopic prophecies had come to pass. The time from submission to the states and ratification had been only 3 months and 8 days the shortest time in which an Amendment has been ratified.

FELON DISENFRANCHISEMENT

There remained one major barrier to universal suffrage: the disenfranchisement of prisoners and ex-prisoners. According to the Sentencing Project, prisoners cannot vote in 48 states; 31 states deny voting rights to those on probation and 35 disenfranchise parolees. In 13 states, a felony conviction effectively results in a *lifetime* ban on voting. Only two states allow inmates to vote.

Other democracies do not restrict voting rights of citizens who commit crimes. Indeed in 2005, the European Court of Human Rights held that a blanket ban even on voting from prison violates the European Convention on Human Rights, which guarantees the right to free and fair elections.

In 1974 the U.S. Supreme Court, in still another display of American Exceptionalism ruled that states could strip felons of the right to vote even after they had come out of prison and completed their probation and parole. In a cruel irony the Court used a passage in the 14th Amendment, an Amendment adopted to give former slaves equal protection and citizenship rights, to justify a decision that has stripped millions of blacks and Hispanics of the foundation of citizenship—the right to vote.

From 1980 to 2010 the prison population expanded almost fivefold to 2.2 million. The population on probation rose to 4.06 million. Today over 7 million adults are on probation, parole or in jail or prison. If we include ex felons who have served their sentences, the total could be 20 million.

The burden of these laws falls disproportionately on blacks and Hispanics. Approximately 13 percent of the United States' population is African American, yet African Americans make up 38 percent of the prison population. Slightly more than 15 percent of the United States population is Hispanic, but they comprise 20 percent of the prison population.

By 2014, Florida, Kentucky and Virginia disenfranchised 20 percent or more of black adults. Overall, one of every 13 blacks has lost the right to vote.

In the national elections of 2012 all state felony disenfranchisement laws added together blocked an estimated 5.85 million people from voting, up from 1.2 million in 1976.

A careful analysis by Professors Christopher Uggen and Jeff Manza suggests that disenfranchising felons has altered the American political landscape. After the 1984 elections, for example, Republicans held a 53-47 Senate majority. If felons had been allowed to vote Democrats probably would have been elected to the Senate in Virginia, Texas and Kentucky.

Mitch McConnell likely would never have become Majority Leader. In 1984 candidate McConnell narrowly defeated the Democratic nominee by 5,269 votes. The total number of disenfranchised felons in Kentucky that year was over 75,000. Using a very low presumed ex-prisoner voter turnout rate of 13 percent, almost 11,000 Democratic votes likely were lost to disenfranchisement, twice the Republican plurality.

Florida disenfranchises 1.5 million voters, the highest rate in the nation. In the 2000 election, George W. Bush won the Florida election, and therefore the Presidency, by 537 votes. Again using an extremely low turnout rate an additional 60,000 net votes for Gore would have swept him into office.

Samuel Alito and John Roberts would not be Supreme Court Justices. The death of Antonin Scalia would not be convulsing the nation.

Felon disenfranchisement is clearly a partisan issue. Today 12 states deny voting rights to some or all ex-felons who have successfully completed their prison, parole or probation terms: Alabama, Arizona, Delaware, Florida, Iowa, Kentucky, Mississippi, Nebraska, Nevada, Tennessee, Virginia and Wyoming. Eight of these went red in the 2012 Presidential election.

On July 4, 2005, to mark Independence Day, Democratic Governor Tom Vilsack issued an executive order restoring voting rights to Iowans who had completed sentences for felonies. In the nearly six years it was in effect, Vilsack's order restored voting rights to an estimated 115,000 citizens. On Inauguration day, January 14, 2011, Republican Governor Terry Branstad reversed that order.

In 2007 then Republican Governor Charlie Christ of Florida instituted streamlined procedures to restore voting rights to ex-felons. More than 150,000 citizens had their rights restored. In 2011 Republican Governor Rick Scott narrowly edged out Christ, who was running as an Independent and reversed his reforms.

DIRECT DEMOCRACY

The Founding Fathers created a Republic, not a Democracy. They wanted the popular will expressed through elected representatives, not directly. But by the late 19th century people were fed up with representatives they viewed as corrupt and unresponsive. The Populist and Progressive movements arose to channel the people's dissatisfaction. As the advocacy group, Citizens in Charge observes, "The supporters of both these movements had become especially outraged that moneyed special interest groups controlled government, and that the people had no ability to break this control...The cornerstone of their reform package was the establishment of the initiative process for they knew that without it many of the reforms they wanted – that were being blocked by state legislatures – would not be possible."

In 1897 Nebraska became the first state to allow its cities to initiate legislation (initiative) or vote on legislation already passed (referendum). Between 1898 and 1918, 24 more states and even more cities adopted similar provisions. Today 37 states, the District of Columbia and hundreds of cities have initiative and referendum.

Eighteen states also allow the recall of governors, although only once have voters turned out a governor in midterm. Over 60 percent of American cities allow for recall and thousands of local officials have been recalled over the years.

Progressives also challenged the backroom power dealings of political party officials by advocating compulsory statewide primaries. In 1903 Wisconsin introduced such a law. Oregon soon followed. By 1916, the only states in the Union that had not yet adopted a primary system of some kind were Connecticut, New Mexico, and Rhode Island.

PRE-EMPTION

Today, except for felons, the United States has universal suffrage. But recently, states have diminished the value of suffrage by denying local voters the right to vote on specific issues.

In late 2014 the residents of Denton, Texas directly voted to ban fracking. The Texas legislature quickly stripped them and all Texas citizens of the right to vote on that issue. After Madison and Milwaukee raised the minimum wage the Wisconsin legislature preempted them and all cities from doing so. When cities began implementing mandatory sick leave policies seven states banned such policymaking.

Preemption is increasing. "2015 saw more efforts to undermine local control on more issues than any year in history," says Mark Pertschuk, director of the watchdog group Preemption Watch. Legislatures in at least 29 states introduced bills to block local control over a range of issues, from the minimum wage, to LGBTQ rights, to immigration.

In Michigan a new law specifically prohibits local governments from "the regulation of terms and conditions of employment within local government boundaries". That includes wages, sick leave scheduling, and for good measure, the law also prohibits local governments from saying no to big box stores like Walmart.

A bill introduced into the Oklahoma legislature would go further, effectively stripping all Oklahoma cities of home rule. If enacted, local government actions would have to be specifically authorized by the state or they would be invalid.

VOTING RIGHTS UNDER SIEGE

The right to vote matters little if you can't cast your vote. In the last 50 years states have made it ever easier to access the ballot. Today 37 states allow for early voting. Three states allow voting by mail. Eleven states plus the District of Columbia allow for same day registration. States have facilitated military and overseas voting.

And then in 2008 the Supreme Court opened the door to more restrictive voting procedures when it upheld an Indiana law that required all voters casting a ballot in person to present a United States or Indiana photo ID.

The facts of the case were not in dispute. Those least likely to have state-issued identification are disproportionally poor and nonwhite. The only voter fraud addressed by photo IDs is voter impersonation fraud, which is practically nonexistent.

Nevertheless, by a 6-3 vote the Supreme Court declared Indiana's law valid. Justice John Paul Stevens, writing for the majority opined that from then on the burden of proof would not rest on the state to justify new voting restrictions but on the citizenry to prove that this created a burden. And not just an incidental burden As Stevens explained, "Even assuming that the burden may not be justified as to a few voters, that conclusion is by no means sufficient to establish petitioners' right to the relief they seek."

Voter ID, like felon disenfranchisement, is a partisan issue. In 2014 the GAO reported voter ID depresses voter turnout by 1.9-3.2 percent, largely in communities of color and the poor. That helps Republicans. As Nate Silver observes, "In almost every state where the ID laws have been at issue, Republican governors and legislatures have been on the side of passing stricter ones, while Democrats have sought to block them."

Since 2010, 23 states have either introduced more restrictive voter procedures or tightened those in operation.

Arizona passed a law requiring voters to show proof of citizenship, a move that could have a dramatic impact on both voter registration and voter turnout. In June 2013 the Supreme Court ruled it could not do so, but advised Arizona it could sue the Election Assistance Commission, whose four Commissioners are appointed by the President and confirmed by the Senate, to get the federal voter registration form amended to require proof of citizenship in those states that requested the change. Arizona, Georgia and Kansas did so.

In early 2014 the EAC denied their petition. Arizona sued the EAC and in June 2015 the Supreme Court affirmed the authority of the EAC to do so.

On November 2, 2015 the EAC announced the hiring of a new Executive Director. Brian D. Newby had been a Kansas county elections commissioner for 11 years and is a friend of Kansas Secretary of State Kris Kobach. A few days later Kansas, along with Georgia and Alabama sent another petition to the EAC. In late January 2016, without public notice or review by other EAC Commissioners, Newby granted their request, effective immediately.

Events are quickly unfolding. Voting rights groups, backed by a furious Department of Justice, petitioned the District Court to issue a temporary restraining order. In late February the District Court refused to do so, pending a full hearing on March 9.

States are trimming or eliminating measures adopted over the last 20 years to bolster electoral participation by minority and younger voters. Eight states have enacted new laws cutting back on early voting days and hours. In 2013 North Carolina lawmakers reduced early voting days from 17 to 10, ended the ability to register and cast a vote on the same day and abolished a preregistration program for 16- and 17-year-olds.

In 2013 the Supreme Court effectively struck down the heart of the Voting Rights Act of 1965 by a 5-to-4 vote, freeing the nine covered states and dozens of counties in New York, California and South Dakota to change their election laws without advance federal approval. The Department of Justice can still sue under another section of the VRA, something they have done several times since 2013.

The case of Texas illuminates the challenges that remain in achieving effectively universal suffrage.

Texas' photo ID law was first blocked in 2012 under VRA. "A law that forces poorer citizens to choose between their wages and their franchise unquestionably denies or abridges their right to vote," wrote Judge David Tatel. "The same is true when a law imposes an implicit fee for the privilege of casting a ballot."

After the Supreme Court ruling the DOJ again sued Texas. In her October 2014 ruling, Judge Nelva

Gonzales Ramos noted that 600,000 registered voters in Texas—4.5 percent of the electorate—lacked a government-issued ID, but the state had issued only 279 new voter IDs. African-Americans were three times as likely as whites to not have a voter ID and Hispanics twice as likely. She concluded, the law was passed by the Texas legislature, "*because of* and not merely *in spite of* the voter ID law's detrimental effects on the African-American and Hispanic electorate." She called it a "poll tax" and enjoined Texas from putting the photo ID law into effect.

Five days after Ramos issued her ruling, the US Court of Appeals for the Fifth Circuit—one of the most conservative courts in the country—lifted the injunction. The Supreme Court upheld the Appeals Court.

As part of her decision Judge Ramos remarked, "In every redistricting cycle since 1970, Texas has been found to have violated the VRA with racially gerrymandered districts." In 2016 the Supreme Court will hear still another case involving Texas voter laws. This one involves apportionment.

Texas wants to take an unprecedented step: reapportioning based on the number of eligible voters not the total voting population. This would have devastating impacts on communities of color. About a third of the Hispanic population are under 18 compared to less than a fifth of the white population. About a fifth of Hispanics are adult non-citizens compared to a minuscule number of whites. If the proposal were to go into effect, in other words, it would take almost 2 Hispanic votes to equal one white vote.

A lower court denied Texas the right to put this new voting apportionment scheme into effect. It is possible the

Supreme Court would have approved it by a 5-4 decision, but with the death of Scalia the lower court's ruling will be in effect.

Despite the Supreme Court decisions that made one-person one vote the law of the land, states continue to gerrymander election districts. All parties do so but recently the Republican Party has elevated gerrymandering to a fine art. As a result in Pennsylvania, Ohio and Virginia one Republican vote equals 2.5 Democratic votes. In North Carolina the ratio is 3 to 1. In 2008 California citizens exercised their initiative rights to create an independent redistricting Commission to redraw election districts. An independent assessment found that the process has elicited broad bipartisan support and resulted in many more competitive legislative races.

The Founding Fathers had an elitist vision of governance that Americans in the 20th century disavowed. But democracy is a fragile flower. Untended its roots wither. Recently we have not been good gardeners. Perhaps as a result democracy is now under siege. It is up to an engaged citizenry to honor those who have given their lives over the last century to achieve universal suffrage by protecting and expanding the franchise in the face of concerted attacks by monied power.

1. While the Supreme Court has previously stated that it can't determine if partisan gerrymandering has gone too far, the author argues that many cases of gerrymandering reduce the votes of certain political or racial minorities, making it

take two or three votes to equal one vote from the majority. However, Americans are guaranteed one vote per person. Do you think this means that the Supreme Court could have decided on partisan gerrymandering sooner?

2. Explain how gerrymandering makes one person's vote not equal to another person's vote. Use examples from this article as well as others you've read in this book.

"'REVISED' DEMOCRAT MAPS SHOW MORE GERRYMANDERING, LITTLE HISPANIC INFLUENCE," BY KYLE GILLIS, FROM THE *NEVADA JOURNAL*, MAY 25, 2011

DEMOCRATS INCREASE PARTISAN ADVANTAGE IN CONGRESSIONAL DISTRICTS AND BARELY TOUCH HISPANIC POPULATIONS

Lawmakers spent 89 session days drawing their first redistricting maps, but Assembly Democrats managed to produce "revised" maps only three days after Republican Gov. Brian Sandoval vetoed the first set.

Assembly Democrats introduced their new maps—in AB566—Tuesday, May 17 during an Assembly

Legislative Operations and Elections committee meeting. They then passed them in the Senate and Assembly committees by party-line votes.

The maps included revised voting-age populations for 28 Assembly districts, all 21 Senate districts, and the four congressional districts.

"Based on floor statements, based on talks of deviations, [and] based on the governor's veto, we made changes," said Assembly Speaker John Oceguera, D-Las Vegas, during the meeting.

Despite the population revisions, most of the Hispanic-influenced districts remain unchanged, meaning the revised Democrat maps still contain fewer Hispanic-influenced districts than do the Republican maps. Each party has accused the other of potentially violating the federal Voting Rights Act.

The Democrats' original maps contained two Hispanic-majority Assembly districts and one state Senate district. The original maps reduced the number of Hispanic-majority Senate districts from the current number but kept the same number of Hispanic-majority Assembly districts.

In their revised plan, the Democrats retain two Hispanic-majority Assembly seats from their original plan (Assembly Districts 11 and 28), and add a second Hispanic-majority Senate seat (Senate District 10). The new plan increases from 12 to 13 the number of Assembly districts with a Hispanic voting-age population greater than 25 percent. The number of such Senate districts remains unchanged at six.

Some of the biggest changes in the new plan were in the new congressional districts, with the current district of Rep. Shelley Berkley, a Democrat, now stretching into Esmeralda, Lincoln and Lyon counties, and Republican Rep. Joe Heck's district remaining wholly in Clark County.

While the district shapes changed, the Hispanic voting-age numbers in each district remained nearly identical to the original plan. The Hispanic voting-age population in CD-3, now represented by Heck, increased from 24.69 percent in the first plan to 31.33 percent in the revised one, while the comparable percentage in CD-1 (Berkley) dropped from 28.71 to 22.29. The Hispanic voting-age populations in Congressional Districts 2 and 4 changed by less than 0.3 percentage points.

"It's hard to see any major changes or envision a different end result," said Assemblyman Pat Hickey, R-Reno, during the May 17 meeting. By "end result," he indicated, he was referring to a Sandoval veto.

Hickey also criticized the lack of quality debate concerning the Democrat and Republican map alternatives.

"Our [Republican] map wasn't really heard in this committee," Hickey said. "I disagree [with Assembly Speaker Oceguera] and don't think we've had any real conversations at this point."

Democrats countered they wouldn't give the Republican map a hearing because Republican map data hadn't been released on public mapping systems. On May 20, the Republicans released their data and a statement indicating their willingness to compromise.

"Democrats have put forth two plans with info but no Republican [info]," said Assemblyman and committee Chair Tick Segerblom, D-Clark, during the meeting. "If we don't see any data or changes, we're going to go back and forth with party-line votes."

Despite "changes" mentioned by Oceguera, the new plan's lack of Hispanic influence suggests little Democrat attention to the wording in Sandoval's veto statement.

"Of the four Congressional seats it establishes, not one contains a Hispanic majority — though such a district can clearly and simply be drawn, consistent with traditional redistricting principles," Sandoval had written. "The representation of the Hispanic population would be no more fair in the State Senate and Assembly plans, where most Hispanics are crowded into as few districts as possible and where those that are not constitute overwhelming minorities in the districts they are in."

Sandoval also charged political gerrymandering, writing: "This plan ensures partisan opportunity rather than the fair representation of all Nevadans. Partisan gerrymandering is not legal, equitable, or acceptable."

Assembly Democrats' revised maps do enhance their partisan advantages.

Originally, the maps offered by the Democrats gave their party three Democrat-leaning districts (CDs 1, 3 and 4), while CD-2 retained a Republican advantage. In their revised maps, the Democrats padded or maintained their advantages in CDs 1, 3 and 4 while decreasing the Republican advantage in CD-2. Registered Democrats remained at 47 percent in CD-1, increased from 35 to 36 percent in CD-2 and increased from 44 to 47 percent in CD-3. In CD-4, registered Democrats decreased from 43 to 42 percent, but registered Republicans remained at 35 percent, thus maintaining a Democrat advantage.

The configuration of the proposed new Democrat congressional districts would benefit several of their rumored congressional candidates, including Senate

Majority Leader Steven Horsford, D-Clark, Sen. Mo Denis, D-Clark, and Oceguera. The newly proposed CD-1, with a 47 percent-to-31 percent registered-Democrat advantage, encompasses Horsford's current state Senate district. Oceguera's current district straddles CDs 3 and 4, which are both Democrat-leaning districts. Additionally, the current state Senate district represented by Denis is within CD-3, which also contains the largest Hispanic voting-age population (31 percent).

Denis, Horsford and Oceguera are each members of their respective chamber's Legislative and Operations committee.

If approved, CD-3 would become the most heavily Democrat district in the state (17-percentage-point Democrat advantage). Currently held by Rep. Heck, it would likely make his re-election campaign extremely difficult.

"The congressman expects the state legislators to do their job, but he'd hope in the [redistricting] process they'd put Nevadans above politics," said a spokesman from Heck's office.

Hickey challenged the Democrats' political motives and questioned whether the Democrats' call for "public input" was simply a charade.

"Can you [Legislative Counsel Bureau and Assembly Democrats] show where public plans were incorporated into the amendments?" Hickey asked. "It's not a public process if we aren't incorporating public suggestions."

If Sandoval vetoes the revised maps, it's uncertain whether the Democrats will pursue a third bill in the remaining two weeks of the session. Segerblom told the Nevada News Bureau last week, "There is no Plan C."

Sandoval's office has not indicated whether the governor would make redistricting the topic of a special session, as was the case in 2001, or if he'll allow the issue to be resolved judicially. Both parties, expecting a stalemate over the maps, have filed placeholder lawsuits.

1. The redistricting discussed in the article potentially violates the Voting Rights Act because of how Hispanic voters are redistricted. Do you believe the redistricting in this article is an instance of gerrymandering? Explain.

"OPINION: TIME FOR SUPREME COURT TO LIMIT GERRYMANDERING," BY MICHAEL COLLINS, FROM MARYLANDREPORTER.COM, MARCH 25, 2018

The U.S. Supreme Court on Wednesday is scheduled to hear Benisek v. Lamone in what could be a landmark decision for — or against — political gerrymandering. The decision will either inflame or temper partisan passions, but in either case, will shape the nation for generations to come.

Benisek v. Lamone is similar to the Whitford v. Gill case heard by the court last October. While each case makes technical arguments about whether inferior courts applied precedents or interpreted laws properly, both cases turn on the question of whether redistricting based on party affiliation unfairly tramples a citizen's First Amendment right to freedom of association.

MARYLAND CASE

Benisek stems from the 2012 redistricting which specifically targeted Maryland's 6th Congressional District in an attempt to flip it from Republican to Democrat. In order to do that, hundreds of thousands of voters were moved into and out of the 6th District in order to make it more winnable by Democrats.

The plaintiff sued but the U.S. District court refused to hear the case, and refused to let it be heard by a three-judge panel. The Fourth Circuit also refused to hear the case. The Supreme Court (SCOTUS) ruled that they at least deserved a hearing and that led to some interesting discovery.

WISCONSIN CASE

Whitford v. Gill was similarly intriguing but referred to state legislative districts. Republicans took control of the Wisconsin legislature for the first time in generations and controlled redistricting in 2011. They did so with a vengeance, moving district lines such that in 2012, even though Republicans legislators only got 48% of the vote, they took 60 of 99 seats in the legislature, while in 2014, they got 63 of 99 seats while winning 52% of the vote.

Maryland Democrats are equally insufferable in redrawing state legislative districts. They routinely mix single- and multi-member districts to advantage Democrats. For example, after legislative District 31 in the Pasadena area of Anne Arundel County became reliably Republican, it was split into districts 31a and 31b in order to carve a Democratic seat from a Republican district.

In neighboring District 32, however, all members run at large in a majority Democratic district, thereby claiming all three delegates seats for the Democrats.

In addition, Maryland allows a 10% population difference in state districts, and most Democratic-leaning districts have fewer voters than Republican ones.

This helps give Democrats a 3-to-1 advantage in the legislature despite only a 2-to-1-voter registration advantage. That power was then used to redraw congressional districts to give Democrats a 7-to-1 advantage over Republicans.

REDISTRICTING CHALLENGES

Federal District and Appellate Courts have played an interesting role. Federal courts typically do not hear challenges to redistricting based upon claims of discriminating against party affiliation. Since Elbridge Gerry first carved up Massachusetts for partisan advantage in 1812, courts have recognized partisan redistricting as a power granted state legislatures by the Constitution.

The need to break up Jim Crow offered a path for judicial intervention in redistricting. The Voting Rights Act of 1965 outlawed racial gerrymandering that diluted minority voting power. However, this gave legislative mapmakers both a sword and a shield for more partisanship—especially when combined with Big Data and computers.

Republicans often packed as many minorities into a district—ostensibly to comply with the Voting Rights Act. Not coincidentally, this also made districts solidly Democrat, thereby weakening Democrat power in other districts while preserving and advancing minority representation.

CRITICAL PERSPECTIVES ON GERRYMANDERING

Democrats were equally cynical in racial gerry-mandering. They packed as many minorities into the heart of Republican districts to split it—making the district or multiple districts, vulnerable to Democratic challengers. These tactics are called "packing and cracking."

PARTISAN COURTS

During his two terms in office, President Obama sought to reorient the nation by shifting the balance of power in appellate courts. The traditionally conservative Fourth Circuit Court of Appeals, which hears cases from Maryland, Virginia, and North Carolina, was packed with liberal jurists. Thus, the Fourth Circuit became more aggressive in redistricting cases—but only in Republican controlled states.

The Fourth Circuit court, for example, ordered Virginia and North Carolina to redraw districts to help Democrats. At the same time, it refused to hear the Benisek case or challenges to Maryland's Third Congressional District, which has been called the most gerrymandered district in the nation.

More recently, the Pennsylvania Supreme Court made up of five Democrats and two Republicans—all elected—voted along party lines to order that Pennsylvania's congressional map be redrawn to the advantage of Democrats.

With such judicial activism in left-leaning courts, judicial restraint by conservative jurists is a suicide pact. While conservative jurists defer to gerrymandering in states like Maryland, liberal jurists show no such restraint and order new district boundaries in states like North Carolina to help out Democrats—heads, we win, tails, you lose.

HOPE FOR THE FUTURE

SCOTUS has a rare opportunity to create a blueprint for the nation to follow on both federal and state legislative districts. The court can use the Whitford and Benisek cases to denounce partisan gerrymandering by Republicans and Democrats in both state legislative districts and congressional districts.

By setting strict parameters on compactness, contiguousness, minimal allowable differences in district population, etc., the court can erect guardrails to help steer our politics away from the gutters and more to the center—perhaps restoring some civility to our body politic.

While the court rightfully should be wary that such rules would enmesh the courts in future redistricting fights, it needs to be clear-eyed—they are already there. Kicking the can on this issue is a fool's errand. The Whitford and Benisek cases give SCOTUS the choice either to act now, or react forever. The choice is clear.

1. The author notes that other courts who have heard gerrymandering cases have decided based on partisan ideals. How do you think this impacts the likelihood of others to continue gerrymandering? Do you think this makes it more important for the US Supreme Court to decide a partisan gerrymandering case? Explain why or why not.

2. Racially based gerrymandering was outlawed in the 1960s, but the author suggests that this opened up the doors for partisan gerrymandering instead. Do you agree with this suggestion? Using examples from the author's article and other articles in the book explain your reasoning.

"GAPS, GUARDRAILS AND THE FAST-ADVANCING MATH OF PARTISAN GERRYMANDERING," BY SCOTT GORDON, FROM *WISCONTEXT*, DECEMBER 21, 2017

The arguments driving a potentially landmark court case over partisan gerrymandering in Wisconsin may already be outdated.

Argued before the U.S. Supreme Court in October 2017 and due for a decision by June 2018, the lawsuit *Gill v. Whitford* centers around several different mathematical formulas that attempt to quantify the effects of redistricting on voters' rights in a representative democracy. One prominent aspect of the case is a concept called the the efficiency gap, which quantifies the difference between the partisan makeup of the popular vote and the partisan makeup of the winning candidates across a number of legislative districts. Those ballots cast that do not contribute to the election of a given

WHAT THE MEDIA SAY

candidate are known as "wasted votes," with that figure and the total number of votes used to calculate the efficiency gap figure.

The creators of the efficiency gap propose a formula that determines whether a party's candidates received more wasted votes in a given legislative election. If votes for one party's candidates are wasted to a level that sufficiently exceeds another's, that may be evidence that partisan gerrymandering has gone too far. Proponents of the efficiency gap test aren't necessarily saying it should be impossible for one party or another to have an advantageous map of legislative districts — they're saying there's a measurable point at which maps are so skewed that they make competitive elections impossible and violate the principle of one person, one vote.

However, the Supreme Court has generally held that politically-motivated gerrymandering is constitutional, as long as it's not racially discriminatory. While justices have at times inveighed against it, the Court has no standard for intervening when a district map merely creates a partisan advantage. Justice Anthony Kennedy, who plays an instrumental role as a swing vote on the court, has hinted in previous cases that he'd be open to a partisan-oriented standard. But as of 2017, nothing in the case law even offers justices a road map for determining when a party has gone too far in redistricting to its own advantage. Formulas like the efficiency gap are one response to this challenge.

THE LIMITS OF A SIMPLE CALCULATION

Among a community of mathematicians who coalesced around catching and curbing partisan gerrymanders, the efficiency gap has already taken a backseat.

Moon Duchin is a Tufts University mathematics professor who has played an instrumental role in organizing that community through her own research and an ongoing series of conferences. She respects the scholarship behind the efficiency gap, but also sees the formula as limited.

"I think that the efficiency gap is doing about as good as a job as possible at capturing everything in one number, but that's where I think the problem is," Duchin said.

Calculating the efficiency gap for a given legislative map will yield a score, but for Duchin and her peers, "gerrymandering is just too rich," mathematically speaking, to be boiled down that simply.

"I would argue that *Whitford* was off by one year from the computer sampling revolution," Duchin said, referring to the rise of a different approach in gerrymandering research. "Which is such a bummer because we waited 30 years for a big partisan case to go up before the Supreme Court."

Jordan Ellenberg, a University of Wisconsin-Madison math professor, co-organized one of Duchin's conferences in Madison in October 2017, and has written a *New York Times* op-edon the science of gerrymandering. He sees a high efficiency gap as a "red flag." But he doesn't see the test as a basis for a constitutional standard that guides when courts can send state legislators back to the drawing board.

"It would not be a good idea to impose or advocate a legal standard where if your efficiency gap is above a certain threshold, that's unconstitutional," Ellenberg said.

One of the efficiency gap's toughest critics is Wendy K. Tam Cho, a University of Illinois political science professor with a particular interest in statistical and mathematical models. In a July 2017 essay for the *University of Pennsylvania Law Review*, she broke down how the efficiency gap falls short in its attempt to measure electoral unfairness on partisan grounds.

The efficiency gap test measures all votes cast for losing candidates as wasted, as well as all votes for winning candidates beyond the number needed to ensure a majority, and in the exact same way.

"In the efficiency gap measure, both excess winning votes and losing votes are considered the same, but waste needs to be defined by its context," Cho wrote.

Because the efficiency gap test equates different kinds of waste, it can perversely reflect well on a district map that's in fact politically skewed. In an email interview, Cho explained the problem this way: "If Republicans win a district 75 percent to 25 percent, then the Republicans have wasted 25 percent and the Democrats have wasted 25 percent. This would be deemed optimal by the efficiency gap because both parties waste the same number of votes. A situation where a district is that lopsided is clearly not optimal."

Another objection Cho makes is that the efficiency gap tries to factor in the underlying partisan composition of the population, though partisanship is a mutable characteristic with no set definition. A registered Republican or Democrat won't always follow the party line ideologically and won't always vote strictly along party lines, so measuring by party preference doesn't cut it, she says. One could define a district or precinct or state's partisan measure based on how it voted in a previous congressional or presidential election, but those votes can swing, sometimes dramatically so. Plus, as Cho points out, being fair to political parties is a very different thing from being fair to the electorate.

A MULTIPLICITY OF REDISTRICTING POSSIBILITIES

Legislative redistricting combines principles of geometry and demographics, so the practice does lend itself to quantifying outcomes in order to determine fairness. Mathematicians and political scientists have worked in the past to understand, for instance, the compactness of districts and this factor's role in elections. A geographically contorted district clearly is not compact, but is it possible to measure how compact it is compared to how compact it could be? Is it proportional? Is it representative? Does it keep communities of interest intact?

Moon Duchin and other scholars who study the math of redistricting want to develop better methods for understanding gerrymandering and drawing fairer maps. One goal of Duchin's conferences is to equip more academics to serve as expert witnesses in a flurry of redistricting lawsuits that shows no signs of abating. These mathematicians are talking about the efficiency gap, but they're thinking much more about an entirely different approach to detecting excessive partisan gerrymanders.

A plaintiff challenging a partisan gerrymander in court could use a calculation like the efficiency gap to argue that a legislative district map puts a certain group of voters at an unfair disadvantage. Or the plaintiff could use software to generate dozens or thousands or even millions of possible legal ways to draw that map, and place the existing one within the vast continuum of options. Researchers who advocate for this method call it the "sampling" approach.

Rather than put a number on how politically skewed a district map is, sampling places that map within the context of a bunch of different possibilities.

"What [sampling is] good at is telling you if one proposed plan is way out of whack with the rest of the alternatives," Duchin said.

She sees an emerging consensus among gerrymandering-focused mathematicians that the best approach is to construct algorithms using what's known as Markov chain Monte Carlo methods to generate massive numbers of legislative district maps with minor variations between them, while also accounting for already established legal constraints and generally agreed upon qualities that district maps should have.

Computing power has made gerrymandering far more sophisticated and politically effective, with people who seek to carve up specific portions of the electorate to their own advantage already benefiting from such advances. The stage legislatures that undertook redistricting after the 2010 Census had access to sophisticated mapping software of a kind that just hadn't existed in previous cycles. Such software can use not only Census data to draw potential districts, but can also factor in other demographic or political data, enabling those in power to fine-tune their maps for optimal advantage while still obeying the letter of the law.

A majority party drawing new districts to give itself political advantage might have a lot of complex data to take into account, but it ultimately only needs to come up with one map, not thousands. Perhaps the power of computing can also be used to check lawmakers who try to pick their voters too selectively. And this approach will indeed require tremendous amounts of computing power.

"If you think about it in terms of all the choices that you make when you're drawing a districting map, it's an unthinkable more than astronomical number of choices for how to take a state like Wisconsin and take its wards and divides them up into districts. You can't even think about the space of all the possibilities," Duchin said in an Oct. 3, 2017 interview with Wisconsin Public Radio's *Central Time*.

WHAT THE MEDIA SAY

HOW COMPUTING CAN AND CANNOT HELP

The conversation around sampling didn't really reach a critical mass until *Gill v. Whitford* was already up and running through the court system, so it was not and won't be much help to the Wisconsinites challenging the redistricting at issue in that case.

In court, scholars can cross-reference batches of sampled maps with voting data to show what election outcomes they might likely yield, and where the challenged map fits into the continuum of possible outcomes. A group of researchers at Duke University did exactly this to understand how the Wisconsin Assembly district maps the state created in 2011 Act 43 may have altered election results and by extension the balance of power in the state.

"What'll happen out of those millions of possibilities is you'll get a bell curve that shows all the diff ways it could turn out," said Moon Duchin on *Central Time*. "And then you look at Act 43, at the current assembly plan, and you'll see it's all the way out on the tail of the bell curve. It's not in the fat part, it's an outlier."

This observation reflects what Duke University researcher Jonathan Mattingly and colleagues found in a September 2017 paper that used sampling to compare Wisconsin's post-2011 Assembly district maps with nearly 20,000 other possibilities. By cross-referencing every potential map with votes in several recent state legislative elections, Mattingly found that the current

189

Assembly districts favor Republican candidates much more strongly than most other possible maps.

Researchers using voting numbers from previous elections are also working on ways to account for the fact that some elections are uncontested, and that the specific demographics and partisan leanings of districts will affect the makeup of candidates and parties' strategies in specific races. But even with these factors in mind, Mattingly believes his work shows that gerrymandering in and of itself can play a demonstrable role in shifting election outcomes and therefore the partisan composition of legislatures.

"Let me say this with big stars around it: one disturbing thing to me is how much the outcomes shift just by drawing reasonable maps," Mattingly said. "If an equally deciding factor is how the maps were drawn to who voted and how, it does give me pause."

In addition to analyzing the Wisconsin Assembly districts, Mattingly has testified in a North Carolina gerrymandering lawsuit that has some parallels to *Gill*.

"Some people want to ask, well, are we really simulating alternate realities?" he said. "In some sense, whenever somebody asks you to do diagnostics, what they're really asking you to do is compare this reality to some other reality."

By using voting data from actual elections, available demographic data, and relevant legal constraints on redistricting, Mattingly and other sampling practitioners try to hew as close to reality as they can in such an exercise.

University of Illinois political scientist Wendy K. Tam Cho has been using the school's Blue Waters supercomputer to develop a highly sophisticated map-sampling algorithm called PEAR.

"I think what is important, especially for the mathematicians, is that applying math usefully and well to this problem requires a depth of domain knowledge," said Cho. "If people are serious about working on the problem, they should spend the time to learn the case law, how court cases work, understand the history, learn about the political process, et cetera. There are many moving parts here."

Advocates of sampling are not proposing that states adopt computer-generated district maps. State legislatures have the constitutional authority to draw maps as they see fit, within the bounds of case law and both state and federal statutes.

Duchin and her colleagues also respect the fact that redistricting often must factor in messy political and other human factors. For instance, in some states, drawing maps to provide a certain degree of protection to incumbents is considered entirely legitimate. Voters of one ideological bent or another are often clustered together, like left-leaning voters in big cities, so a district drawn to be compact may not be competitive in a strictly partisan sense. And sometimes there's a statutorily defined reason for a strangely shaped district — Illinois' 4th Congressional district, often dubbed the "earmuffs" district, is drawn to ensure that Chicago's large but geographically dispersed Latin American population is represented in a majority district. Even the most sophisticated algorithm paired with the mightiest super-computer cannot generate a one-size-fits-all approach.

"There's no legal or historical basis for taking the power to draw maps away from the legislature," Duchin said. "It's not how we do elections. But giving them some sort of guardrail or guideline — that's completely legitimate, or well within the purview of the courts as we've seen when one person one vote was articulated."

The hope of mathematicians who research gerrymandering is that sampling can take more specific conditions into account, because it's more flexible than a purely abstract score like the efficiency gap. An algo-rithm powerful enough to create thousands of perfectly legal district maps can also incorporate all sorts of parameters specific to a state and various localities.

The scholars tackling cutting-edge problems related to gerrymandering also expect a lot of tough questions from the courts as more plaintiffs use sampling to challenge legislative maps. Duchin anticipates that because the number of possible redistricting maps in a given state is astronomically large, a judge might reason-ably ask whether a sample of, say, 20,000 is really all that representative of the acceptable possibilities.

"That's a pretty good question mathematically and legally, and I hope that's the level of debate that we see in the courts," Duchin said.

"Gaps, Guardrails and the Fast-Approaching Math of Partisan Gerrymandering" was originally published on WisContext, which produced the article in a partnership between Wisconsin Public Radio, Wisconsin Public Television and Cooperative Extension.

1. The author talks about the ways in which redistricting is done when it is done correctly. After reading how it's done, discuss how you would determine what your area's voting districts should be. Do you think the voting map for your area has been drawn well?

2. There are two views on efficiency gaps presented in this article. Based on the arguments presented, do you think the efficiency gap should continue to be a key in how districts are redrawn?

CHAPTER 6

WHAT ORDINARY CITIZENS SAY

Ordinary citizens are the ones most affected by gerrymandering, but it's not often we hear their opinion on the subject. The media, as you saw in the previous chapter, focuses on what politicians and those in power have to say, while the courts and government focus on the perceived impact on everyday people. But we don't get to hear what people like us think. In this chapter, you'll read articles from people who are not part of the fight for or against gerrymandering but who are impacted by it and want to express their thoughts.

"FAIR ELECTIONS, RIP," BY EMILY SCHWARTZ GRECO AND WILLIAM A. COLLINS, FROM *OTHERWORDS*, JUNE 26, 2013

Voting rights are under attack again — this time it's the Supreme Court's turn.

The majority's ruling in the *Shelby County vs. Holder* case gutted key Voting Rights Act provisions at a time when minority access to the polls faces new obstacles.

As Justice Ruth Ginsburg explained and proved in her dissent, the law is working well but remains necessary. She likened the ruling to "throwing away your umbrella in a rainstorm because you are not getting wet."

But not everyone is peeved. The decision cheered up any Republican leaders who remained sour that their hospitality to the far-right fringe came back to bite them last November.

In what's turning into a tradition, tea-partying enthusiasts forced rabid Senate candidates onto the ballot in 2012. Some of them lost what might have been easy wins when they turned out to be too radical for the general public.

Then there's the White House. Despite spending a record $1.2 billion to win the presidency, Mitt Romney and the GOP blew that race.

Yes, the GOP did hang onto its majority in the House of Representatives. But Republicans now only have a 33-seat edge on the competition in that chamber, down from the 49-seat margin they enjoyed before the 2012 elections.

Now, you might guess these great leaders would move swiftly to rebrand the GOP to appeal to more voters. Or distance their party from those vote-repelling tea partiers. Well, guess again. They've settled on a different strategy: cheating.

An earlier Supreme Court ruling helped make this new approach possible. Remember that *Citizens United* decision? It allowed corporations for the first time to buy directly into elections with unlimited contributions.

The Republicans found out in November, when Romney outspent Barack Obama by more than $100 million, that it will take more than gobs of corporate cash to win big.

But money is only one GOP angle. Another is fraud. No, no, not that Republicans will vote twice or anything so pedestrian.

Instead, they accuse poor people of voting fraudulently, and thereupon get legislatures to pass laws making voting a serious hassle if you're not part of the in-group with a government-issued photo ID. Republican operatives are also fond of flyers and announcements that threaten insecure new citizens and poorly educated voters with arrest if their papers are not exactly in order.

Another voting deterrence tool is inconvenience. Other nations — and many states — have long worked to increase polling places, lengthen voting hours, stimulate mail balloting, and simplify procedures.

Contrarily, numerous Republican-controlled states are seeking to reverse all those trends. The GOP's theory is simple enough: We know who poorer, less mobile people tend to vote for, and it isn't us. Hey, let's make it as hard for them to vote as we can.

Yet another tactic is gerrymandering. State legislatures normally draw boundaries not only for their own districts but for Congress as well. In some states, lawmakers exert this power mainly to protect their own personal seats.

Ginsburg calls these tactics "second-generation barriers to minority voting." Thanks to that shiny new Supreme Court ruling, they're now easier to pull off.

Now the Republican Party, wherever it's in charge, is going further. It's crowding Democratic voters, especially around urban centers, into a few contorted pockets. This practice spreads the Republican voters around, helping the GOP accumulate additional "safe" legislative and congressional seats.

The GOP's creative redistricting explains why President Obama won Wisconsin by more than 200,000 votes while Democrats only carried three of the state's eight congressional districts.

There's more. Coming soon to a gerrymandered state near you: an attack on presidential elections.

Here's how this trick works: Each state gets to determine how its own electoral votes will be allocated — either by a statewide "winner-take-all" system or by congressional district. Republican-gerrymandered states are moving quickly to distribute their electoral votes by congressional district.

Isn't that convenient? Even if the Republican Party doesn't need any more help from the Supreme Court, our democracy sure does.

1. The authors accuse Republicans of gerrymandering and suggest that the Republican Party is the only one guilty of bad voting acts. Based on the cases you've read in this book, list three ways that other political groups have impacted voting districts.

2. Gerrymandering is cited as just one of many ways political parties are trying to steal votes and disenfranchise American voters. Do you believe gerrymandering is equivalent to the other problems mentioned by the authors? Explain.

"GERRYMANDERING: HOW OUR ELECTIONS ARE REALLY RIGGED — PART ONE," BY BERNIE O'HARE, FROM *LEHIGH VALLEY RAMBLINGS*, AUGUST 30, 2016

Do any of you know what gerrymandering is? Put in its simplest form, it's a process by which our legislators pick the voters instead of the other way around. It takes place every ten years, after the census. Though it's almost unnoticed, it is probably the biggest danger to our representative democracy. It's a rigged system, designed to provide job security for legislators who toe the line while punishing any who dare rebel. The fox is in the henhouse, as politicians themselves decide on new districts. They can extend their stay as long as they want. It has resulted in a Pennsylvania State legislature that is completely unresponsive to voters. And it's getting worse.

On Friday night, at the Unitarian Universalist Church in Bethlehem, a large group of nearly 100 people attended a gerrymandering panel discussion that included Pa LWV Board member Carol Kuniholm, State Sen. Lisa Boscola (Dem.), State Rep. David Parker (Rep.) and Common Cause PA's Barry Kauffman. Boscola and Parker have teamed up with bi-partisan legislation to fix a broken system, but they will be the first to tell you nothing is going to happen unless voters themselves get involved and start pressuring their own legislators. In addition, leaders like House Democrat Frank Dermody and Republican Speaker Mike Turzai, who have been unwilling to act, need to be targeted.

Today's focus is the problem of gerrymandering itself, as laid out by Kuniholm. Tomorrow, I'll get into the bi-partisan legislative fix proposed by Boscola and Parker. Thursday, I'll tell you what wizened reformer Barry Kauffman thinks about the problem. Friday, I'll finish with what our local legislators are doing, or more accurately, not doing.

Every time there's a poll of Pennsylvania voters, the issue that bothers them the most is school district funding. Most people think the state should contribute more, and less money should be coming out of their pockets in the form of increased property taxes. They want a fairer way to fund schools, and one that keeps seniors on fixed incomes in their homes. And of course, there has been a rash of bills over the years to change the way schools are funded. Lisa Boscola herself has for years been a champion of property tax reform. But it always fails. It will continue to fail, too. That's because legislators no longer serve you.

Though gerrymandering has existed since the 1800's, there was a big change in the 2012 election cycle. "Something went crazy," says Kuniholm.

First, a new mapping technology called Maptitude provides locations of candidates and incumbents, census information, economic information and precinct-by-precinct reports of election results in previous elections. It's just the thing to have to draw a district so that a preferred candidate wins.

Second, technology and computing power has made for a vast increase in data mining capabilities over the past ten years that Kuniholm calls the "difference between a horse and buggy and a rocket ship."

The third big change is money. In the wake of Citizens United, hybrid Super PACs have provided a huge infusion of undisclosed outside money that is then used to win elections. It can't be traced.

Both parties have these hybrid SuperPACs.

REDMAP2010

For Republicans, it is RedMap2010, which dumped $30 million into state races to affect the redistricting, with the ultimate goal being control of the US Congress through reapportionment.

Republicans admit this. They were able to buy Pennsylvania for just a little under $1 million in 2010, despite having fewer votes than Democrats. Here's what they themselves say:

> "[T]he RSLC [Republican State leadership Committee] spent nearly $1 million in Pennsylvania House races in 2010 – an expenditure that helped provide the GOP with majorities in both chambers of the state legislature. Combined with former Republican Attorney General Tom Corbett's victory in the gubernatorial race, Republicans took control of the state legislative and congressional redistricting process. The impact of this investment at the state level in 2010 is evident when examining the results of the 2012 election: Pennsylvanians reelected a Democratic U.S. Senator by nearly nine points and reelected President Obama by more than five points, but at the same time they added to the Republican ranks in the State House and returned a 13-5 Republican majority to the U.S. House."

Things went so well that Republicans are raising $125 million for the 2020 redistricting, four times what they spent in 2010.

By winning control of the state legislature, they were able to insure a nearly three to one advantage in Congress, despite having less numbers

ADVANTAGE 2020

Before you get too upset at those evil Republicans, I have to tell you Democrats are now doing the same thing with a hybrid SuperPAC called Advantage 2020. They are focused on Pennsylvania, and have the 6th Pa. Congressional District featured on their homepage. This SuperPAC blasts the gerrymandering done by the GOP, but that's precisely what they want to do, too.

Kuniholm failed to say how much money Democrats intend to raise, but it has to be substantial.

The money spent by both parties has nothing to do with you. It is all about flipping districts to win control of the state legislature and, ultimately, Congress. He who controls the state legislature, controls redistricting. He who controls redistricting controls Congress.

International groups on both sides contribute to these SuperPACS, so far all we know, China and Russia could be buying the Democrat or Republican Party

FOCUS IS WINNING AND CONTROL, NOT EFFECTIVE GOVERNANCE

This enhanced gerrymandering has resulted in a significant change in state government. The focus is winning and control instead of effective governance. Legislators who rebel and want to work for the common good end up being targeted or ignored.

The political agenda is no longer what is right for the people, but is instead held hostage to outside moneyed influence. "That money that's pouring in is much more than what is being raised locally by the legislators," said Kuniholm. "There's a lot of research that shows that once that outside money comes into an election, the loyalty of those who are elected has shifted. They are no longer loyal to the constituents, who did not put them in office. They are loyal to the outside interests that put them in office."

At the same time, the extremes within the party of a safe district become the norm, leading to disaffection by everyone else. So nationally, 43% of Americans refuse to declare themselves with either party. In Pa, only 13% are independent, but that is only because primaries are closed.

"There's basically no effective choice," noted Kuniholm. To drive that point home, she said that 86% of our state incumbents had no primary challengers this year. For the general, 57% have no opposition.

"How do you vote them out if nobody's running against them?" she asked.

1. The author notes that the major political parties are spending money on redistricting or gerrymandering in order to win elections and take control of Congress. Do you think this is a problem the way the author does? Explain using examples from this and other articles.

2. In addition to money, the author blames the advances in digital mapping technology for the increase in gerrymandering in the twenty-first century. Do you think the technology being blamed for the problem could help create a less controversial redistricting plan, or can having that much data only lead to misuse?

CONCLUSION

The United States is a representative democracy, which means every citizen over the age of eighteen has a right to vote and to have their vote counted. Gerrymandering, however, prevents people from having their votes counted and their voices heard. When representatives redraw district lines to create a more favorable voting pool, they're doing so at the expense of certain American voters.

As you've learned, not all redistricting is an act of gerrymandering, but there's a very fine line between the two. When there is gerrymandering, there are a number of reasons someone made that choice. Sometimes districts are gerrymandered to give one political party favor over another, or redistricting is done to keep one group of people—a political party, a race, a nationality, or a religious group—from having power in the voting booth. It's done to win elections or to keep the other side from winning. And even when it doesn't seem all that bad, it's preventing citizens from enacting their right to have a say in how their government is run.

But is gerrymandering as big a problem as it seems? And is it always harmful? If you've read the articles in this book carefully, you should have come to your own conclusions about what gerrymandering does to American democracy.

BIBLIOGRAPHY

Altman, Micah, and Michael McDonald. "The Voting Rights Act." PublicMapping.org. Retrieved May 23, 2018. http://www.publicmapping.org/what-is-redistricting/redistricting-criteria-the-voting-rights-act.

Bass, Gary D., and Danielle Brian. "Draining the Swamp: A How-To Guide." *OtherWords*, December 14, 2016. https://otherwords.org/draining-the-swamp-a-how-to-guide.

Collins, Michael. "Opinion: Time for Supreme Court to Limit Gerrymandering." MarylandReporter.com, March 25, 2018. http://marylandreporter.com/2018/03/25/opinion-time-for-supreme-county-to-limit-gerrymandering.

Collins, William A., and Emily Schwartz Greco. "Fair Elections, RIP." *OtherWords*, June 26, 2013. https://otherwords.org/fair-elections-rip.

Daley, David. "A Supreme Court Case Could Make Partisan Gerrymandering Illegal." BillMoyers.com, October 2, 2017. https://billmoyers.com/story/supreme-court-case-make-partisan-gerrymandering-illegal.

Daley, David. "The Real Way the 2016 Election Is Rigged." BillMoyers.com, *Common Dreams*, August 21, 2016. https://www.commondreams.org/views/2016/08/21/real-way-2016-election-rigged.

Drutman, Lee. "Funny Shapes Aren't the Problem with American Voting." *New America*, February 11, 2016. https://www.newamerica.org/weekly/110/funny-shapes-arent-the-problem-with-american-voting.

Duchin, Moon, and Peter Levin. "Rebooting the Mathematics Behind Gerrymandering." *The Conversation*, October 23, 2017. https://theconversation.com/rebooting-the-mathematics-behind-gerrymandering-73096.

Duros, Staci. *Gill v. Whitford: Wisconsin's Partisan Gerrymandering Case*. Wisconsin Legislative Reference Bureau, 2017. https://docs.legis.wisconsin.gov/misc/lrb/elections_information/gill_v_whitford.pdf

Eberly, Todd. "Redistricting Should Restore Representative Democracy." MarylandReporter.com, September 29, 2015. http://marylandreporter.com/2015/09/29/redistricting-should-restore-representative-democracy.

Entin, Jonathan. "Is Partisan Gerrymandering Illegal? The Supreme Court Will Decide." *The Conversation*, September 27, 2017. https://theconversation.com/is-partisan-gerrymandering-illegal-the-supreme-court-will-decide-84241.

Gillis, Kyle. "'Revised' Democrat Maps Show More Gerrymandering, Little Hispanic Influence." *Nevada Journal*, May 25, 2011. http://nevadajournal.com/2011/05/25/revised-democrat-maps-show-more-gerrymandering-little-hispanic-influence.

Gordon, Scott. "Gaps, Guardrails and the Fast-Advancing Math of Partisan Gerrymandering." *WisContext*, December 21, 2017. https://www.wiscontext.org/gaps-guardrails-and-fast-advancing-math-partisan-gerrymandering.

Hutchins, Corey. "Redistricting in Colorado: Clearing Hurdles, Looming Court Fight, Pick Ups and Putdowns." *The Colorado Independent*, December 8, 2017. http://www.coloradoindependent.com/167813/redistricting-coloroado-gerrymandering-fair-districts.

Johnson, Jake. "'Victory for Democracy' as Court Rules Against North Carolina Gerrymandering." *Common Dreams*, January 10, 2018. https://www.commondreams.org/news/2018/01/10/victory-democracy-court-rules-against-north-carolina-gerrymandering.

Lopez, Soyenixe. "Arizona Voters Can Overrule Legislature on Redistricting, High Court Says." *Cronkite News*, June 30, 2015. https://cronkitenews.azpbs.org/2015/06/30/arizona-voters-can-overrule-legislature-on-redistricting-high-court-says.

Morris, David. "America's Long (and Unfinished) Road to Democracy." *Commons Magazine*, November 12, 2016. http://www.onthecommons.org/magazine/americas-long-and-unfinished-road-to-democracy#sthash.1Fu1saQV.dpbs.

O'Hare, Bernie. "Gerrymandering: How Our Elections Are Really Rigged." *Lehigh Valley Ramblings*, August 30, 2016. https://lehighvalleyramblings.blogspot.com/2016/08/gerrymandering-how-our-elections-are.html.

Sajtewrj8. "Former AG Holder Blasts Georgia Redistricting 'Power Grab.'" *Sajja News*, March 15, 2017. https://sajja.news/former-ag-holder-blasts-georgia-redistricting-power-grab.

Sandbrink, Andrea. "Achtung! Voter Suppression Is Coming to Europe." HEINRICH-BÖLL-STIFTUNG, November 2017. https://us.boell.org/2017/11/01/achtung-voter-suppression-coming-europe.

US Supreme Court. *Davis v. Bandemer, 478 U.S. 109 (1986)*. June 30, 1986. https://supreme.justia.com/cases/federal/us/478/109/case.html.

US Supreme Court. *Ruth O. SHAW, et al., Appellants v. Janet RENO, Attorney General, et al.* June 28, 1993. https://www.cengage.com/politicalscience/book_content/0547216386_miroff/primary_sources/assets/hmps_shaw_v_reno.html..

CHAPTER NOTES

CHAPTER 3: WHAT THE COURTS SAY

DAVIS V. BANDEMER, 478 U. S. 109 (1986) BY THE US SUPREME COURT

1. Politically speaking, the State of Indiana is a "swing" State: it has supported both the Democrats and the Republicans at various times, often following national trends and major candidates. Although at times within the last few decades the State has voted up to 56% Democratic, in 1980, the Republicans took the State.

2. These bills were "vehicle bills" — bills that had no real content. Both bills were passed and were then referred to the other House, and eventually to a Conference Committee, which consisted entirely of Republican members. Four Democratic "advisers" to the Committee were appointed, but they had no voting powers. Further, they were excluded from the substantive work of the Committee: the Republican State Committee funded a computerized study by an outside firm that produced the districting map that was eventually used, and the Democratic "advisers" were not allowed access to the computer or to the results of the study. They nevertheless attempted to develop apportionment proposals of their own, using the 1980 census data. A few days before the end of the 1981 legislative session, the Conference Committee presented its plan to the legislature. The Democratic minority also presented its alternative plan. The majority plan was passed in both Houses, with voting along party lines, and was signed into law by the Governor.

3. A multitude of conflicting statistical evidence was also introduced at the trial. The District Court, however, specifically declined to credit any of this evidence, noting that it did not "wish to choose which statistician is more credible or less credible." 603 F. Supp., at 1485.

4. The court noted that various House districts combined urban and suburban or rural voters with dissimilar interests, and that many of the districts were unwieldy shapes. Using Marion County

as one example, the court observed that the county itself had
exactly the population to support 14 House seats; nevertheless,
it was combined with various surrounding areas to form five
triple-member districts, which maintained the county's prior
15-member delegation even though it had in fact suffered a population decrease. Believing that the resulting multimember districts
were suspect in terms of compactness, the court concluded that
no rational reason could support them.

5. In addition, the court quoted from the deposition testimony of
the Speaker of the House as follows:

"MR. SUSSMAN: What I would like you to do here again
is to give me whatever reasons were operative to your
mind in maintaining or creating multimember districts
with regard to (Districts) 48 through 52 [the Marion
County districts]."

"MR. DAILEY: Political."

"MR. SUSSMAN: What were the political factors?"

"MR. DAILEY: We wanted to save as many incumbent
Republicans as possible."

Id. at 1484.

The court also quoted from the deposition testimony of
Senator Bosma as follows:

"MR. SUSSMAN: This (newspaper) article says further,"

"Under further questioning from Townsend about input
in actual map drawing, Bosma said 'You will have the
privilege to offer a minority map. But I will advise you in
advance that it will not be accepted.' Is that accurate?"

"MR. BOSMA: That's accurate. I might add that I don't
make goals for the opposite team."

Ibid.

6. These are familiar techniques of political gerrymandering.
Democratic (or Republican, as the case may be) votes are
"stacked" and "wasted" by creating districts where Democrats

form majorities much greater than the 50% necessary to carry those districts. Concurrently, Republican votes are spread among districts in which they form safe, perhaps 55%, majorities, and Democratic votes are "cracked" or "split" by dispersing them in such a way as to be ineffectual.

7. Judge Pell, writing in dissent, disagreed. Assuming for the purposes of his analysis that a political gerrymandering case was justiciable, he concluded that the appellees had not proved discrimination. Rather, once the relative voting strengths were properly ascertained, it was his view that the plan had advantaged and disadvantaged both parties equally: the Democrats won more than their voting strength in the Senate and less in the House. *See id.* at 1501-1502. Judge Pell also rejected the majority>s analysis of the multimember districts, and thought that the State had followed rational, nondiscriminatory criteria in formulating the 1981 plan.

8. Consolidated with this suit in the proceedings below was another lawsuit, filed by the Indiana NAACP. The NAACP suit challenged the plans as unconstitutional dilutions of the black vote in Indiana in violation of the Fourteenth and Fifteenth Amendments and the Voting Rights Act of 1965, 42 U. S. C. §1973 (as amended).
In rejecting the NAACP claims, the District Court majority found: "[T]he voting efficacy of the NAACP plaintiffs was impinged upon because of their politics, and not because of their race. It is not in dispute that blacks in this state vote overwhelmingly Democratic." 603 F. Supp., at 1489-1490. Consequently, the majority found no Fifteenth Amendment or Voting Rights Act violation. The dissent concurred with this result, but gave different reasons for reaching this conclusion.
The NAACP did not appeal these dispositions. Consequently, the only claims now before us are the political gerrymandering claims.

9. As to the illegitimate policy determinations that JUSTICE O'CONNOR believes that we have made, she points to two. The first is a preference for nonpartisan, as opposed to partisan, gerrymanders, and the second is a preference for proportionality.

On a group level, however, which must be our focus in this type
of claim, neither of these policy determinations is "of a kind
clearly for nonjudicial discretion." *Baker v. Carr,* 369 U. S. 186,
369 U. S. 217 (1962). The first merely recognizes that nonpartisan
gerrymanders in fact are aimed at guaranteeing, rather than
infringing, fair group representation. The second, which is not a
preference for proportionality *per se,* but a preference for a level
of parity between votes and representation sufficient to ensure
that significant minority voices are heard and, that majorities
are not consigned to minority status, is hardly an illegitimate
extrapolation from our general majoritarian ethic and the
objective of fair and adequate representation recognized in
Reynolds v. Sims, 377 U. S. 533 (1964).

10. This passage from *Gaffney* expresses a view similar to that
    of Robert G. Dixon, Jr., one of the foremost scholars of
    reapportionment, who observed:

    "[W]hether or not nonpopulation factors are expressly
    taken into account in shaping political districts, they are
    inevitably ever-present and operative. They influence
    all election outcomes in all sets of districts. The key
    concept to grasp is that there are no neutral lines for
    legislative districts . . . every line drawn aligns partisans
    and interest blocs in a particular way different from the
    alignment that would result from putting the line in
    some other place."

Dixon, Fair Criteria and Procedures for Establishing Legislative
    Districts 7-8, in Representation and Redistricting Issues (B.
    Grofman, A. Lijphart, R. McKay, & H. Scarrow eds.1982).

11. That discriminatory intent may not be difficult to prove in this
    context does not, of course, mean that it need not be proved at
    all to succeed on such a claim.

12. Although these cases involved racial groups, we believe that
    the principles developed in these cases would apply equally to
    claims by political groups in individual districts. We note, how-
    ever, that the elements necessary to a successful vote dilution
    claim may be more difficult to prove in relation to a claim by

a political group. For example, historical patterns of exclusion from the political processes, evidence which would support a vote dilution claim, are in general more likely to be present for a racial group than for a political group.

13. Although this opinion relies on our cases relating to challenges by racial groups to individual multimember districts, nothing herein is intended in any way to suggest an alteration of the standards developed in those cases for evaluating such claims.

14. The requirement of a threshold showing is derived from the peculiar characteristics of these political gerrymandering claims. We do not contemplate that a similar requirement would apply to our Equal Protection cases outside of this particular context.

15. The District Court apparently thought that the political group suffering discrimination was all those voters who voted for Democratic Assembly candidates in 1982. Judge Pell, in dissent, argued that the allegedly disfavored group should be defined as those voters who could be counted on to vote Democratic from election to election, thus excluding those who vote the Republican ticket from time to time. He would have counted the true believers by averaging the Democratic vote cast in two different elections for those statewide offices for which party-line voting is thought to be the rule and personality and issue-oriented factors are relatively unimportant. Although accepting Judge Pell's definition of Democratic voters would have strongly suggested that the 1981 reapportionment had no discriminatory effect at all, there was no response to his position. The appellees take up the challenge in this Court, claiming that Judge Pell chose the wrong election years for the purpose of averaging the Democratic votes. The dispute need not now be resolved.

16. It should be noted that, even if the District Court correctly identified constitutional shortcomings in the House districting, this did not automatically call for invalidating the provisions for the Senate. The only relevant fact about the Senate appearing in

the District Court's findings is that, in the 1982 elections to fill 25 Senate seats, Democrats won 53.1% of the statewide vote and elected 13 of their candidates. That, on its face, is hardly grounds for invalidating the Senate districting, and we have counselled before against striking down an entire apportionment statute when the constitutional evil could be cured by lesser means. *Whitcomb v. Chavis*, 403 U.S. at 403 U. S. 160-161.

17. Although JUSTICE POWELL asserts that we mischaracterize these cases, and that any effects in addition to disproportionality were required to be demonstrated only to prove discriminatory intent, we note that the effects test we cite was initially set forth in *White v. Regester*, 412 U. S. 755 (1973), which was decided before the Court expressly determined that proof of discriminatory intent was a necessary component of an equal protection claim. Moreover, the Voting Rights Act, which to a large extent borrowed the effects test from *White*, explicitly declined to require any showing of discriminatory intent. It may be true that our more recent cases have turned on the question of discriminatory intent, but that does not imply that we have abandoned the effects discussion we adopted earlier. Moreover, we believe that JUSTICE POWELL incorrectly asserts that more than one election must pass before a successful racial or political gerrymandering claim may be brought. *Post* at478 U. S. 171-172, n. 10 (concurring in part and dissenting in part). *Projected* election results based on district boundaries and past voting patterns may certainly support this type of claim, even where no election has yet been held under the challenged districting.

18. JUSTICE POWELL proffers additional election results from the 1984 elections in support of his conclusion. These results were not considered by the District Court, and we decline to determine their significance without the benefit of any factual development as to their meaning in terms of Democratic power overall or in the long run. Nevertheless, we note that, in terms of actual percentages, the 1984 House election results cited by JUSTICE POWELL exhibited less of a discrepancy between Democratic votes cast and Democratic representatives elected than did the 1982 results (5% as opposed to 8%). This casts at least some doubt on the import of the 1982 results.

19. In most equal protection cases, it is true, a discriminatory effect will be readily apparent, and no heightened effect will be required, *see* n 14, *supra*, but that is the only real difference between this type of equal protection claim and others.

20. Thus, we have rejected none of the District Court's subsidiary factual conclusions. We have merely, based on our view of the applicable law, disregarded those that were irrelevant in this case, and held insufficient those that inadequately supported the District Court's ultimate legal conclusions. Specifically, we have not rejected the District Court's finding of discriminatory intent. Nor have we rejected the District Court's findings as to any of the election results or the contours of particular districts. We have simply determined that, aside from the election results, none of the facts found by the District Court were relevant to the question of discriminatory effects. Consequently, since we did not need to progress beyond that point, given our conclusion that no unconstitutional discriminatory effects were shown as a matter of law, we did not need to consider the District Court's factual findings on the other "factors" addressed by JUSTICE POWELL.

21. Although we recognize the difficulty of this inquiry, we do not share JUSTICE O'CONNOR's apparent lack of faith in the lower courts' abilities to distinguish between disproportionality *per se* and the lack of fair representation that continued disproportionality in conjunction with other indicia may demonstrate. *See post* at 478 U. S. 157(opinion concurring in judgment).

22. We are puzzled by JUSTICE POWELL's conclusion that we contemplate a test under which only the "one person, one vote" requirement has any relevance. This opinion clearly does not adopt such a limited review.

"PARTISAN GERRYMANDERING AND ITS FOUNDATIONAL CASE LAW" BY STACI DUROS

64. The other eleven plaintiffs are Roger Anclam, Emily Bunting, Mary Lynne Donohue, Helen Harris, Wayne Jensen, Wendy

Sue Johnson, Janet Mitchell, Allison Seaton, James Seaton, Jerome Wallace, and Donald Winter.

65. Beverly R. Gill, Julie M. Glancey, Ann S. Jacobs, Steve King, Don Mills, and Mark L. Thomsen.

66. The term "gerrymander" was first used in the *Boston Gazette* on March 26, 1812, and created in reaction to a redrawing of the Massachusetts Senate election districts under the governor, Elbridge Gerry. When mapped, one of the districts was said to resemble the shape of a salamander. Gerrymander is a portmanteau of the governor's last name "Gerry" and the word "salamander."

67. Partisan gerrymandering can be used interchangeably with political gerrymandering.

68. This example assumes that the urban voters would vote differently than the suburban voters.

69. A *majority-minority district*, also known as a *minority opportunity district*, is an electoral district in which the majority of the constituents are racial or ethnic minorities. Majority-minority districts have been the subject of legal cases examining the constitutionality of such districts, including *Shaw v. Reno*, 509 U.S. 630 (1993); *Miller v. Johnson*, 515 U.S. 900 (1995); and *Bush v. Vera*, 517 U.S. 952 (1996).

70. Two cases will be discussed in detail within the main body below, for they set the precedent of the rationale to challenge cases as unconstitutional under the Fourteenth Amendment's equal protection clause and "one person, one vote" principle as well as the First Amendment rights of freedom of speech and association, cf. *Davis v. Bandemer*, 478 U.S. 109 (1986) at 122–3; Vieth v. Jubelirer, 541 U.S. 109 (2004) at 314 (Justice Kennedy, concurring in judgment) ("penalizing citizens because of their participation in the electoral process, . . . their association with a political party, or their expression of political views") (citing *Elrod v. Burns*, 427 U.S. 347 (1976) (plurality opinion)).

71. *Fortson v. Dorsey*, 379 U.S. 433 (1965). A federal district court had held unconstitutional a multimember district system in Atlanta (Fulton County) in which the seven-man delegation to the state senate was elected at large in the county on a winner-take-all basis, even though technically each legislator was assigned to a subdistrict in the county. This system would make it more difficult for minorities to elect representatives in proportion to their voting strength on a regular basis. While the Supreme Court reversed the district court's decision for lack of proof of inequity, Justice Brennan said, "It might well be that, designedly or otherwise, a multimember constituency apportionment scheme, under the circumstances of a particular case, would operate to minimize or cancel out the voting strength of racial or *political* elements of the voting population" (id. at 439) (emphasis added).

72. Burns v. Richardson, 384 U.S. 73 (1966) at 88–99. This case involved the reapportionment of the Hawaii Senate and is somewhat of an outlier from the other cases in this group because Hawaii's geography heavily affects the drawing of boundaries. The case also deals with the question of voter eligibility, including the large numbers of the military population, especially on the island of Oahu, as well as if fluctuating numbers of tourists in the reapportionment process can pass constitutional muster, (id. at 94–6).

73. *White v. Regester*, 412 U.S. 755 (1973) at 766.

74. *Gaffney v. Cummings*, 412 U.S. 735 (1973).

75. *Id*. at 754.

76. In *Davis v. Bandemer*, 478 U.S. 109 (1986), the Supreme Court held that partisan gerrymandering was a justiciable issue, but ruled that a violation of the equal protection clause by the Republican-controlled Indiana Legislature had not been proven.

77. *Bandemer v. Davis*, 603 F. Supp. 1479 (S.D. Ind. 1984) at 1492–1495. The district court relied heavily on *Karcher v. Daggett*, 462 U.S. 725 (1983), a challenge to a New Jersey congressional plan that allegedly diluted Republican voting strength in

Newark, as well as *City of Mobile v. Bolden*, 446 U.S. 55 (1980), a challenge on racial discrimination that generated a discriminatory purpose test for violations of the equal protection clause.

78. *Id.* at 1495.

79. Davis v. Bandemer, 478 U.S. 109 (1986) at 113. Claims that are considered to be "justiciable" are those that are able to be adjudicated by a court. Justice O'Connor, joined by Chief Justice Burger and Justice Rehnquist, concurred with the majority's decision by declaring that alleged partisan gerrymandering claims are political questions and therefore nonjusticiable. (O'Connor stated that when there is "'a lack of judicially discoverable and manageable standards for resolving it,' or where 'the impossibility of deciding without an initial policy determination of a kind clearly for nonjudicial discretion' is apparent," then the question is political and nonjusticiable.") (*Id.* at 148 (quoting *Baker v. Carr*, 369 U.S. 186 (1962) at 217)).

80. Plurality: Justices Byron White (parts I, III, IV), joined by William J. Brennan, Thurgood Marshall, and Harry Blackmun.

81. *Davis v. Bandemer*, 478 U.S. 109 (1986) at 127.

82. *Id.* at 132.

83. *Id.* at 129.

84. *Id.* at 132.

85. Majority: Byron White (part II), joined by William J. Brennan, Thurgood Marshall, Harry Blackmun, Lewis F. Powell, Jr., and John P. Stevens. Concurrence: Warren E. Burger and Sandra Day O'Connor, joined by Warren E. Burger and William Rehnquist. Concur/Dissent: Lewis F. Powell, Jr., joined by John P. Stevens.

86. *Davis v. Bandemer*, 478 U.S. 109 (1986), at 129–36; see *Vieth v. Jubelirer*, 541 U.S. 267 (2004), at 279–81 recounting the eighteen-year history of litigation under Bandemer and observes that no partisan gerrymandering claim had succeeded in this period.

87. *Id.* at 132–3. 88. Justice White in his plurality opinion in *Davis v. Bandemer*, 478 U.S. 109 (1986), at 127–43.89. Unequal population violates the federal "one person, one vote" principle.

90. Justices Antonin Scalia, William Rehnquist, Sandra Day O'Connor, and Clarence Thomas, with Anthony Kennedy concurring in judgment. Justice Scalia wrote the plurality opinion. It was a split decision that had no majority opinion.

91. *Vieth v. Jubelirer,* 541 U.S. 267 (204) at 281.
92. Justices John Paul Stevens, David Souter, and Stephen Breyer; each justice provided dissenting opinions.

93. *Vieth v. Jubelirer*, 541 U.S. 267 (204) at 307–8.

94. *Id.* at 314–5.

95. *Cox v. Larios*, 542 U.S. 947 (2004); *Johnson-Lee v. City of Minneapolis*, No. 02-1139, 2004 WL 2212044 (D. Minn. Sept. 30, 2004); *Kidd v. Cox*, No. 1:06-CV-0997-BBM, 2006 WL 1341302, 2006 (N.D. Ga. May 16, 2006).

96. In *LULAC v. Perry*, 548 U.S. 399 (2006), the Supreme Court affirmed the district court's dismissal of the statewide political gerrymandering claims and the District 24 Voting Rights Act claim, reversed and remanded the district court's dismissal of the District 23 Voting Rights Act claim, and vacated the district court's race-based equal protection and District 23 partisan gerrymandering holdings because the Court failed to reach them.

97. Majority: Justices Kennedy (in part), joined by Stevens, Souter, Ginsburg, Breyer (Parts II-A & III); Roberts, Alito (Parts I & IV); Souter, Ginsburg (Part II-D); Concurrences: Roberts, joined by Alito; Stevens, joined by Breyer (Parts I, II); Scalia, joined by Thomas; Roberts, Alito (Part III); Souter, joined by Ginsburg; Breyer.

98. Justice Kennedy was joined by Justices Stevens, Souter, Ginsburg, and Breyer in the opinion that partisan gerrymandering cases are justiciable; *LULAC v. Perry*, 548 U.S. 399 (2006) at 447,

483, and 491. Justices Roberts and Alito reserved their judgment on the justiciability (Id. at 492). Justices Scalia and Thomas reiterated their opinion previously expressed in Vieth that partisan gerrymandering claims are nonjusticiable (*id*. at 511).

99. *LULAC v. Perry*, 548 U.S. 399 (2006) at 413–17.

100. *LULAC v. Perry*, 548 U.S. 399 (2006) at 418.

101. *Id*. at 419.

102. *Id*. at 420.

GLOSSARY

conservative — Typically applies to members of the Republican political party and refers to someone who holds traditional values, often related to family and religion.

Democrat — A member of the Democratic Party. Generally, Democrats are believed to be socially and fiscally liberal.

district — A geographic area that is represented by a person or persons in their state and federal government. Districts are represented by their congressmen and congresswomen in the United States House of Representatives.

Electoral College — A group of people who are responsible for electing the president of the United States. Electors are appointed from each state based on population, and each elector is supposed to represent their districts in their vote for president.

gerrymandering — The act of drawing district lines so that a particular district is rigged to have more or less voting power than another district. This is typically done to promote a particular political party, though it can also be done to make sure a specific race or social class has more electoral power.

jurisdiction — An area, either of law or geography, over which a particular governing body has power. For example, the state of New York is under the jurisdiction of the New York governor as well as the United States federal government, while Canada is a separate jurisdiction.

legislature — The body that governs a particular region, be it local, state, or federal.

liberal — This term typically applies to members of the Democratic political party and refers to someone who is open to social change as well as fiscal support of the lower classes, and who believes in the separation of church and state.

minority district — A legislative district in which the majority of the citizens are non-white or ethnic or racial minorities.

partisan — Strong support of a particular political party or cause. "Partisan" is often used in the negative, to refer to situations in which party affinity is problematic, such as in "partisan gerrymandering."

party—A political group made up of people who have the same social, fiscal, or legislative ideals.

redistricting—The act of redrawing district lines. Districts are typically redrawn every ten years, to reflect new data from the United States Census.

Republican—A member of the Republican Party. Generally, Republicans are believed to be socially and fiscally conservative, and they often believe that religion has a place in politics.

suffrage—The right to vote.

suppression—In terms of voting rights, when voters are intimidated or discouraged from voting in order to influence the outcome of an election.

Voting Rights Act—Signed into law in 1965, the Voting Rights Act was enacted to help African Americans and other minorities gain better access to the electorate and to prevent voter suppression.

FURTHER READING

BOOKS

Berman, Ari. *Give Us the Ballot: The Modern Struggle for Voting Rights in America*. New York, NY: Picador, 2015.

Burgan, Michael. *The Voting Rights Act of 1965: An Interactive Adventure*. North Mankato, MN: Capstone Press, 2015.

Lappe, Frances Moore, and Adam Eichen. *Daring Democracy: Igniting Power, Meaning, and Connection for the America We Want*. Boston, MA: Beacon Press, 2017.

McGann, Anthony J., Charles Anthony Smith, Michael Latner, and Alex Keena. *Gerrymandering in America: The House of Representatives, the Supreme Court and the Future of Popular Sovereignty*. New York, NY: Cambridge University Press, 2016.

Miller, William J., and Jeremy D. Walling. *The Political Battle Over Congressional Redistricting*. Lanham, MD: Lexington Books, 2013.

Page, Benjamin I., and Martin Gilens. *Democracy in America? What Has Gone Wrong and What We Can Do About It*. Chicago, IL: University of Chicago Press, 2017.

Rosenfeld, Steven. *Democracy Betrayed: How Superdelegates, Redistricting, Party Insiders, and the Electoral College Rigged the 2016 Election*. New York, NY: Hot Books, 2018.

Roth, Zachary. *The Great Suppression: Voting Rights, Corporate Cash, and the Conservative Assault on Democracy*. New York, NY: Crown, 2016.

Seabrook, Nicholas R. *Drawing the Lines: Constraints on Partisan Gerrymandering in U.S. Politics*. Ithaca, NY: Cornell University Press, 2017.

WEBSITES

The Gerrymandering Project by FiveThirtyEight
http://fivethirtyeight.com/tag/the-gerrymandering-project
This political news website focuses on data and research. The
  Gerrymandering Project looks at redistricting in the United
  States, whether there's a gerrymandering problem, and what
  can be done about it.

The ReDistricting Game
http://www.redistrictinggame.org
Created by the University of Southern California's Annenberg
  Center, this online game allows players to see how redistricting
  is done and attempt redistricting on their own to see how the
  system is used and abused to create gerrymandered districts.

INDEX

ABOUT THE EDITOR

Jennifer Peters is a writer and editor based in Washington, DC. She has written about relationships, politics, defense, the military, books, and the media for such outlets as VICE News, Task & Purpose, and News & Tech. She has written books about addiction, pop culture, and the government, and has edited titles on sports, politics, and the media, including a series on the Islamic State. She always carries a book with her, even when she knows she won't have time to read it.